Foxhead Books

ALSO BY HOWARD L. FEINSTEIN

Developing Issues In The Legal Status Of Women (1999 & 2000 Supplement)

The Amazing Adventures Of Luca And Ceci (2012)

Fire on the Bayou

True Tales from the Civil Rights Battlefront

Foxhead Books

© 2013 by Howard L. Feinstein. All rights reserved.

No part of this document may be reproduced or transmitted in any form or by any means, electronic, mechanical, photocopying, recording, or otherwise, without prior written permission of the author, with the exception of brief exerpts for inclusion in scholarly works or inclusion in reviews. For permissions or further information, post Potemkin Media Omnibus, Ltd. at 140 E. Broadway Ave., Tipp City, O. 45371.

Cover: Christine Lee

Copy Editor: Lynne Frye Bamberger

Feinstein, Howard L.

Fire on the Bayou / by Howard L. Feinstein 206 p. 1.17cm.

ISBN-13 978-1-940876-00-9

This book is dedicated to the memory of Harry and Harriette Moore, and all those others who gave their lives in the struggle for civil rights.

Howard Feinstein is the author of *Developing Issues In The Legal Status Of Women* (Pearson: 1999 and 2000 Supplement), and many legal and social policy articles and materials. He served as a criminal prosecutor and civil litigator with the U.S. Department of Justice, Civil Rights Division. He has taught law and government at the University of Maryland, George Washington University, and Hood College. He received a B.A. from the University of California, and his J.D. With Honors from George Washington University. He studied international and comparative law in the United Kingdom. Howard has served on the boards of Empowered Women International; Congregation Beth Chai; and the Elyse Martin Crosby Domestic Violence Scholarship Fund. He is a performing, recording, and touring rhythm & blues musician. He can be contacted through his website, www.howardlfeinstein.com.

Contents

Author's Note	15
Acknowledgments	17
Prologue: The Horror	19
California Dreaming	27
Hitler at the Post Office	51
All-American City	71
The Long and Winding Road	97
House-Hunting While Black	121
Knights in White Satin	145
The Unforgiven	165
Epilogue: Amazing Grace	191
Coda	199
Notes and Sources	201
A Selected Civil Rights Timeline	209
Applicable Federal Statutes	213

"One day the South will know that when these disinherited children of God sat down at lunch counters, they were in reality standing up for the most sacred values in our Judeo-Christian heritage, thereby bringing our nation back to those great wells of democracy which were dug deep by the founding fathers in their formation of the Constitution and the Declaration of Independence."

Rev. Dr. Martin Luther King, Jr.
Birmingham, Alabama

"You want me to testify against the Ku Klux Klan? You got to be kidding. You're from Washington; you don't know these people. They'll find you in the middle of the night, put you in a flat-bottom boat, take you way out on the bayou, and dump you over. Trust me, nobody'll ever find you."

Ray Sievers
Oakdale, Louisiana

Fire on the Bayou

Fire on the Bayou

Author's Note

This is a work of nonfiction. It recounts certain events which took place during the enforcement stage of the civil rights movement—a period of resurgent Ku Klux Klan activity during an economic downturn. It is also the personal story of what it was like to participate in those events as a young attorney representing the United States. While every effort has been made to document the events described, it is not meant to be a "neutral" account. It is most definitely colored by my feelings about these cases, and about civil rights generally.

All of the events in this book actually took place, to the best of my ability to recall and verify them. All dialogue or quotations are either documented or specifically recalled. Due to the passage of time and imperfect memory, mistakes will surely be discovered—these will be unintentional, but they are my responsibility. Real names are generally used for public officials, judges, and attorneys. The only material departure from adherence to the record is the use of pseudonyms for many private citizens. This is for legal reasons, including privacy and the presumption of innocence. And, even after all these years, one cannot completely discount the possibility of adverse consequences—that's what it was like back then.

This book describes historical events, but the struggle for dignity and justice lives on. For those who wish to support the movement in its current mode—to carry it on, in civil rights parlance: I strongly recommend contributing (tax-deductible) funds and/or time to Empowered Women International. Please visit www.ewint.org.

Howard L. Feinstein

Fire on the Bayou

Acknowledgments

    I would like to thank the following for their kind assistance along the way: Special Agent Fitz Ormon Clarke, FBI, Savannah, GA; Rick Dyson, Acres Home Chamber of Commerce, Houston, TX; Nelson Hermilla, FOIA Branch, Civil Rights Division, U.S. Justice Dept.; Joseph Jarzabek, Assistant United States Attorney, Shreveport, LA; Rev. Wiley F. Shaw, Jr., Bread of Life Christian Center, Oakdale, LA. Ronald P. Bland, Ken Jacobson, Bill Pugh and Isabelle Schoenfeld read all or part of the manuscript, and offered valuable critique. And special thanks to the following for inspiration and support, way beyond the call of duty: Karen Feinstein: True like ice, like fire. Julia Fierro: Superb author and editor, who put me on the right track. Steve Marlowe of Foxhead Books: His faith in this book never wavered. Juanita Evan-

Howard L. Feinstein

geline Moore: Amazing Grace, indeed.

Fire on the Bayou

Prologue—The Horror

"The belief in a supernatural source of evil is not necessary; men alone are quite capable of every wickedness."

Joseph Conrad

In the 1930's and 40's, Florida's north coast was hard, tough country. Jim Crow reigned supreme, and all but a few of his African American subjects lived lives of feudal agricultural and mill labor, often removed from the time of slavery in name only. During the Depression, any job—working in a mill or harvesting oranges, strawberries, or sugar cane—was precious, and could disappear on a whim. Later on, some war industry employment beckoned, but that required a train ride North, and a permanent goodbye to home and family. This was the Old South, hardscrabble Florida, not yet the Space Coast, and a long way from the Gold Coast of Miami.

Florida rarely comes to mind when the story of the civil rights movement is told, but what history there is occurred on the north coast. Some of the fiercest battles in the nation's fight to desegregate public and private facilities—including the Atlantic Ocean beaches—took place in 1963-64 in St. Augustine, America's oldest city. Down the coast in Daytona Beach, on March 17, 1946, Jackie Robinson became the first black professional baseball player of the modern era, taking the field for the Montreal Royals a year before he desegregated the Major Leagues. That game was played at what is now Jackie Robinson Stadium, home to the minor league Daytona Cubs and Bethune-Cookman College's baseball team. As the Depression set in, two graduates of that historically black college, Harry and Harriette Moore, began teaching careers in segregated schools, and started a family, further down the coast in the tiny town of Mims. It is there that they became the first martyrs of the civil rights movement.

Harry Moore wasted little time in challenging the status quo. As a college graduate and professional, he stood tall among his fellow African Americans of the time, but his vision extends far beyond his own well-being. He became a whirlwind of justice and righteousness, decades before the movement that would later sweep the country. By the late 1930's he had established NAACP branches throughout Florida, and served as director of the Brevard County chapter. He filed lawsuits challenging unequal pay for black teachers in the segregated school system. He traveled, with his wife Harriette and their two daughters, all over the state to document and investigate lynchings. He was a force of nature, a one-man threat to the established order, both black and white. He brought Thurgood Marshall and other national figures down to stay at his little house in Mims, and in 1941 he became statewide NAACP director.

In 1944, when the Supreme Court ruled that a state political party cannot restrict voting eligibility to whites only, Harry Moore established the Progressive Voters League, and registered tens of thousands of African American Florida voters, an achievement unheard of elsewhere in the South. This was too much for the all-white Brevard County School Board to swallow, and Moore was removed from his teaching position. Harry Moore's struggle—like that of Marshall, Martin Luther King and others—also represented a challenge to certain segments of the black community, which enjoyed a tacit position of power under segregation. More than a few members of the black clergy leaders feared the uncertain consequences of a movement led by younger leaders less beholden to existing authority. Harry Moore felt the sting of this jealousy when he was eventually removed from his position with the NAACP. A visionary like Moore, beholden to no one but God and his conscience, was the last thing the established order wanted, in a time and place where even incremental change was frightening.

Nothing could stop Harry Moore. In 1949, he took up the notorious case of the Groveland Four, in nearby Lake County, where four black youths were convicted of raping a white woman. The trial was such a travesty of justice that the convictions would be reversed two years later by the Supreme Court. Sheriff Willis McCall, choosing to save the taxpayers the expense of a new trial, shot two of the handcuffed defendants while transporting them to court. Outraged, Moore demanded justice. He spread word of this shocking incident far and wide, and asked the governor and state attorney general to indict Sheriff McCall for murder.

But this was KKK country. The Klan was enjoying a reign of terror in Florida, with at least a dozen bombings already that year. There were no prosecutions, and African American and Catholic churches as well as synagogues laid on extra security. On the north coast, the word went out over the hot-line, accessible to Klansmen, law enforcement officers, clergy, business leaders, and others with a need to know. Special Klavern meetings were held—some attended by Sheriff McCall—and agenda item number one was what to do about Harry Moore, the man who wouldn't back down. The hat was passed. Money was collected. Plans were made. As set forth in official Florida Attorney General's Office findings, Moore was targeted by

> "[e]xceedingly violent members of a Central Florida Klavern of the Ku Klux Klan. High ranking members of the communities, including law enforcement officers, elected officials, and prominent business owners were members of the Klan or shared its beliefs."

This time, Harry Moore had gone too far.

The long-haul train, packed for the holiday season, sped South from Washington, D.C. to Florida, where the Moores' younger daughter, Juanita Evangeline, was to spend the holidays with her family. Like her parents, she too was a Bethune-Cookman graduate, working in the capital for the U. S. Department of Labor, which had just recently begun recruiting black employees. The train would not arrive until two days past Christmas, so the family's presents remained wrapped under the tree, waiting for all to enjoy together. Adding to the joyous occasion, Christmas day also marked the Moores' twenty-fifth wedding anniversary.

When Juanita Evangeline Moore stepped off the train on December 27, 1951, at Titusville, her uncle, a Korean War veteran and one of the first African Americans to serve in the recently-desegregated armed forces, was there to greet her. But he exuded none of the joy of the season, only the bone-weary, heartbreaking look of a man finally given more than he can handle by his God. Where were her parents, asked Evangeline—what had happened?

> *December 25, 1951, 10:20 p.m.:* "*The shades were drawn and the windows to the Moores' house were closed. Christmas music could be heard from outside the house, and the Christmas tree was visible from the woods.*"

The dynamite placed in the crawlspace under Harry and Harriette Moore's bedroom exploded so violently that the little house was lifted off its foundation. The detonation, shattering the peacefulness of the holy night, was heard for miles. Their older daughter, Peaches, was spared only because she slept that night in her sister Juanita's bedroom. The bodies of Harry and Harriette Moore were flung violently upward, through the bedroom ceiling. The souls of these living saints took leave of this Earth, and ascended toward Heaven.

The horror of segregation knows no mercy; there were no exceptions for special circumstances. There was no ambulance service for African Americans. Friends drove the Moores thirty miles to the hospital in Sanford, where Harry Moore was pronounced dead on arrival. Harriette Moore would linger in agony for nine days before succumbing. Florists in Mims did not deliver to "Negro funerals;" flowers were ordered from Miami.

In the immediate aftermath, outrage was widespread. The funeral was moved to a church larger than the Moore family's congregation, to accommodate a gathering of 3,500 people, more than three times the population of Mims. The state offered a reward of $2,000 for information leading to apprehension of the perpetrators. After all, this was hardly the type of publicity that Florida, always dependent upon tourism, needed. Mary McLeod Bethune, founder and president-emeritus of the Moores' alma mater, delivered a passionate indictment of the state's power structure for creating a climate in which such a horror could take place. Bethune, another prophet before her time, left no doubt that while Harry Moore was now with his Maker, his cause remained alive. Illinois Governor Adlai Stevenson, who would soon announce the first of his two presidential candidacies, issued a statement that savagery of this nature tarnished America's image throughout world.

In New York City, widespread messages of protest reached the young United Nations, and a well-attended rally was held, where Langston Hughes read from his new poem, "The Ballad of Harry T. Moore."

And then, for half a century, there was only silence. No arrests. No convictions. Nothing.

Howard L. Feinstein

Fire on the Bayou

California Dreaming

My own days doing battle with the Ku Klux Klan and their brethren continue to haunt me. As Smokey Robinson might say, "they've really got a hold on me." They are in my thoughts, my dreams, my nightmares, my daydreams. When asked "What do you do?" (a standard query in status-conscious Washington), it doesn't take long for me to bring up my old civil rights cases. But it's been over three decades since I "went South." Since then, I've been a government regulatory lawyer, counsel with a law firm, college professor, speaker, author, and musician (no doubt I'll discover my true calling one of these days). Yet I still seem to define myself by my brief but compelling time on the civil rights battlefront.

I am not sure why this is. I don't think of myself as a person who lives in the past. I have less self-reflection than my family and friends. I have shied away from self-analysis, preferring to live by the credo that the unexamined life is not necessarily a bad thing. Yet over and over, to paraphrase Fitzgerald, I beat on, my boat against the current, borne back ceaselessly into the past. In the South, this would be more readily understood. There, where social, economic, and military cataclysms unknown to the rest of the country still resonate, Faulkner, as usual, is right on target: "The past is never dead. It's not even past."

Perhaps this period of personal history lingers out of guilt—for leaving the struggle behind with unfinished business, due primarily to my own shortcomings. Some people stay on the front lines, but not me. I burned out; I backed down. I stamped my return ticket to a less compelling, more predictable life, back in the suburbs with my family. I am hardly the first person to find a return to normalcy to be an awkward, vaguely unfulfilling time of life.

I think of the World War II Resistance agent, portrayed so convincingly by Meryl Streep in the film "Plenty," repeatedly risking her life. After the war, she was never able to recapture that sense of pushing the envelope and learning what she was really made of. I recall research psychologist Kay Redfield Jamison recounting her lifelong battle with manic depression, saying that she would not trade the highs to avoid the lows. The most compelling example of this phenomenon I have ever encountered is the story of holocaust survivor Lenore Hoffman (pseudonym):

> "So I can say of my time in the camps: It was the high point of my life. It sounds strange, but it is so. Of course, I lost my

entire youth, if you want to look at it that way, and a lot of my health, and I don't know what all. But that doesn't outweigh what I gained. I had experiences that one can never have in a bourgeois life, because one is too swaddled in comfort."

Swaddled in comfort. Not a bad description of my own backstory. Looking back, I gradually unearthed clues to my eventual surrender to the magnetic pull of the civil rights arena, but those clues lay well below the surface of my past. I certainly did not grow up with wealth, but I never had to worry about any basic needs. I was under the typically intense, Jewish family pressure to excel academically, but I was lucky not to have to work too hard at it. A bit of a loner, my interests were often outside the orbit of the in-crowd, so I needed an understanding and supportive family—and that I had. I was intellectually and culturally curious, and it was all laid out in front of me for the taking. I wanted to see the world beyond the San Francisco Bay Area, and travel was inexpensive and logistically easy. I was crazy about listening to and performing music, and it was all around me for the taking. What did I know of challenge? What did I know of adversity? One thing I do know: I was in the right place at the right time.

∽

Palo Alto, where I grew up, no longer exists. I was raised in a sleepy college town, home to Stanford University and little else. Today, it is the bustling capital of its own high-tech city-state, Silicon Valley. When I return periodically, to see my dwindling family, I recognize it less and less. This is far from the plight of a home-town past its heyday, eclipsed by economic progress. Far from it—it is a victim of its own success. The area now chokes in the same traffic congestion and smoggy air for which we Northern Californians used to mock Los Angeles. Real estate prices are through the roof. Google, Hewlett Packard, Facebook, and other booming hi-tech employers—nonexistent or mom-and-pop shops in my day—offer special incentives like free transportation and housing subsidies to attract the highly-skilled workers they need.

But there was no Silicon Valley in my youth—just the Peninsula, an agricultural and academic expanse south of San Francisco and north of San Jose, between the ocean and the bay. Palo Alto was its cultural capital, a small community where we knew one another, but also a college town with plenty of intellectual and cultural stimulation from beyond. The center of our world was the family, in classic fifties fashion: I walked to school until tenth grade, and sometimes we ate lunch together—always dinner. Our mothers stayed home; raising a family on one salary was taken for granted. Divorce was something depicted on soap operas. Marriage, we surely believed, was a biological precondition to childbirth.

Our fathers, mostly World War II veterans, were beneficiaries of the G.I. Bill and V.A. housing loans, which propelled them permanently into the middle class. Not that they didn't earn the right to the good life after living through the Depression and the War. My father was often out on the street, stealing food to eat, and he barely survived combat in the Pacific theater. My mother was somewhat better off, but it was all relative in those days. No one questioned the veterans' post-war benefits, which catapulted them into the Great Middle

Class. There was nothing controversial about these massive government affirmative action programs for white males.

Our education, priority number one in just about any Jewish family, was first-rate. My high school could hardly have prepared us better for college. Our teachers and student-teachers were generally from Stanford, right across the street, and we routinely attended lectures and special events there. When I arrived at college, I found that I had already read much of the assigned literature. California's cradle-to-grave, tuition-free, top-rated public education system meant no student loans or extra jobs, a godsend for a family of relatively modest means like mine. We had ready access to public libraries, after-school recreation facilities, museums, swimming pools, and athletic fields galore, within easy walking or bicycling distance. Crime was something one read about in the San Francisco Chronicle—I can still recall the killer's name from my home-town's only murder case.

But that wasn't all. This wasn't just booming, post-war America; this was California! At the height of the Cold War and the Race for Space, the state could barely handle all the huge defense and aerospace contracts that poured in. Highways, schools, colleges, homes, and all the services required by this bonanza were transforming a primarily agricultural, sleeping giant into the economic engine of the country. Jobs, federal and state funds, and opportunity were everywhere. Sonic booms cracked the sky overhead daily, as test pilots striving to be astronauts blasted through the sound barrier. There was little tension between the private and public sectors—both were taking off like rockets. Taxes were still minimal compared with back East, and no one short of the John Birch Society could claim with a straight face that they weren't getting their money's worth back in public services.

We were also rapidly becoming the cultural vanguard of the baby boom generation. San Francisco's Beat Era of the fifties may not have swept the nation, but the musical, political, cultural, and pharmaceutical upheavals of the next decade sure did. When I went East for law school, I fielded endless questions about the rock legends I had played with; the sun and drug-soaked concerts and festivals at Monterey, the Fillmore, the Avalon, and so many other venues; the Free Speech Movement pioneers, Black Panthers, anti-war icons, Rolling Stone writers, hippies, yippies, and fugitive firebrands we'd known as classmates, mentors, and local luminaries; the marches, demonstrations, riots, love-ins, etc. we'd attended; and yes, some high schools and colleges really did have surfing teams. We wanted it all, and we wanted it now! And why not? We were Present at the Creation.

This tableau was not exactly the crucible of the civil rights movement. There was no official, southern-style segregation; no bull-whips or fire-hoses. But there was surely plenty of discrimination—not that it was foremost in our minds. My first personal memory of racial outrage dates back to 1958, when major league baseball came West, another chapter in California's emergence into the big-time. Our newly-beloved Giants, having left New York behind, were greeted with parades, massive media coverage, and joy in the hearts of young sports fans like myself. But when Willie Mays, the ultimate diamond superstar and future Hall of Famer, went house-hunting in San Francisco, skin color trumped celebrity. Mays and his family had trouble finding a seller, and when he finally did purchase a home, it wasn't long before a rock shattered a window. Eleven years old, hardly dreaming that I would one day prosecute similar abominations, I was stunned. What was going on here? This was Willie Mays! My pals and I would give a limb or two to live next door to our idol.

This youthful hero worship of black athletes and musicians, as juvenile and naïve as it sounds today, played no small part in our world, and must have been a subliminal factor in our identification with the underdogs in the civil rights battles of the '60s. In Sunday School, we donated "Trees For Israel" in honor of Roy Campanella and Jackie Robinson—certainly not for Sandy Koufax, the lone Jewish superstar of the era, but a member of the archrival Dodgers. In addition to the revered Mays, the Giants had a long history of signing and promoting minority players. In the fifties, the provincial University of San Francisco, led by the Bay Area's own Bill Russell, brought consecutive collegiate basketball championships to our little corner of the world. A few years later, when professional basketball came to Northern California, the new arrivals were led by, literally, the biggest presence of all in the sports world, Wilt the Stilt Chamberlain. Mays! Russell! Chamberlain! Add to this Chuck Berry, Fats Domino, Ray Charles, and all the other African-American musicians we worshipped and imitated. No one was going to convince us starry-eyed pre-teens of white supremacy.

I can't say I didn't feel the sting of prejudice myself. No community, no matter how well-educated, is entirely free of the values of the greater society, and anti-Semitism was alive, well, and not particularly subtle in those days. Ours was a tiny Jewish community, lacking our own synagogue until much later (my Bar Mitzvah took place in a Unitarian church). No conceivable threat to anyone, highly-assimilated in true California fashion, we still knew where we stood. It was understood that certain places were off-limits—"restricted" was the common term in those days. I was always the only Jew in class, and my elementary and junior high school teachers, to my parents' constant fury, would make sure everyone knew it.

> *Howard, you'll read the part of Shylock. Howard, you didn't bring in a letter from a relative in another country—there must be SOMEONE who's still alive. Howard, tell us what you did for Easter. Howard, don't you know the words to these Christmas carols?*

Granted, an occasional swastika or iron cross drawn on a locker or desk does not constitute a pogrom, but it was tough stuff for a shy junior high kid trying to figure out his place in the social order. I know I never forgot it. As my late mother's best friend put it, reminiscing years later about the good old days, anti-Semitism was the bond that held the neighborhood together. This ignorant bigotry of the times sometimes took comical forms: my close friend, a high school basketball superstar, was occasionally heckled by fans, and even opposing coaches, with anti-Semitic slurs, in the wholly erroneous belief that he was Jewish.

My first concrete action in furtherance of civil rights came at the age of sixteen, when I joined a picket line outside the annual convention of the California Real Estate Association. The realtors were mounting a campaign to overturn the Rumford Act, the pioneering fair-housing law enacted by the state legislature earlier that year. A major figure in this effort was William French Smith—key confidant of our future Governor and President Ronald Reagan, and later U.S. Attorney General, under whom I would later have the dubious distinction to serve. We were surely a motley crew: a few minorities from towns beyond Palo Alto; a contingent of Stanford students and faculty, always up for a good cause; the usual aggregation of liberal housewives with the time to devote to the struggle. Not exactly the children of Birmingham, who were brutalized and jailed just a few months earlier. But every little bit helps.

The Association succeeded in placing Proposition 14, a statewide measure to nullify the Rumford act, on the 1964 ballot, and a heated campaign ensued. The legislature proved wiser than the people, as the initiative passed. But the story was not over. In 1967, in the landmark case of Reitman v. Mulkey, the United States Supreme Court held that a state could not legalize discrimination in violation of the Constitution, and the Fair Housing Act was resurrected. I saved, and still treasure, my tattered bumper sticker from that battle, which reads: Fight Segregation. No On Proposition 14. I still use it as a teaching aid and lecture prop today, a testament to the importance of perseverance in the eternal struggle against discrimination.

I remember another mysterious totem from my early civil rights consciousness. On my boyhood bedroom wall, clipped from some now-defunct magazine—Life? Look? Collier's?—is a chart entitled "Southern Justice." I have no idea why or when I tacked it up, but it stayed there until the day I left for college. It recounted a long, sickening series of cases in which southern Negroes died at the hands of white vigilantes, who were later acquitted by all-white juries. Including such atrocities as the Emmett Till case, it must have represented, to my young, impressionable mind, the Ultimate Evil. I no doubt found it all incomprehensible as a sheltered youth.

But many years later, that chart revisited me in a fever dream, in some stifling Gulf Coast motel room. And it all became clear: of course those old cases were heard by all-white juries, just like the ones I was now trying cases before. Those jurors were selected from the voter rolls, and God knows blacks weren't permitted to vote. Maybe I could do something about that.

I was barely seventeen on my last day of high school. Everyone gathered outdoors for the annual end–of-school memorial ceremony, the bells in the school's massive tower clanging out in recognition of our alumni war dead. But my own life was just beginning. There was no question, thanks to my socioeconomic status, preparatory education, and ethnicity, that college came next. There was no shortage of first-rate, low-cost (indeed, no-cost) institutions in the Bay Area. That would be the easy, logical next step, but that same old centrifugal force of curiosity and adventure was pulling on me again. Leaving the state would have been out of the question; the leading public university system in the country was tuition-free for California residents. I didn't know anyone, other than a couple of football players with athletic scholarships, who would be heading out of state; in fact, many of the best and the brightest from elsewhere in the West would migrate to California. I visited UCLA, but it felt gigantic and overwhelming for a small-town boy like me. Like a kid in the candy store who couldn't go wrong, I settled on the University of California at Santa Barbara, which seemed more my size.

Early one summer morning, a high school friend pulled up in his car (in very un-California fashion, I never owned my own), and I tossed my suitcase into the trunk. My parents were huddled together on our front steps, wiping away tears and reminding me to phone regularly and study hard. My little sister was sleepy and quiet, probably wondering about her new place in the family constellation. But it all seemed natural to me. No worries, no cares—time for the next chapter, ready to take leave of the nest and head on down the road.

⁓

If anything, Santa Barbara, 300 miles down the Pacific coast, seemed even more sun-drenched, laid back, and removed from the great issues of the day than the Peninsula. A few hours after moving into my dormitory room, I was scampering down a cliff to the beach, heading out into the waves on a borrowed surfboard. During "orientation week," my new roommates and I gathered intelligence on (a) the freshman female population; (b) evading the legal drinking age (this will later give way to other substances); and (c) priority number one: finding people to play music with. I'd played with the best up north; time to see what they've got down here. As freshmen, we pursued the standard, grueling 1960s triple major in sex, drugs and rock 'n' roll. My first semester, I set no academic records; I was way too immature to handle all that new-found freedom. From then on, I cruised by on native intelligence and intellectual curiosity. I was nothing if not inconsistent in those days, managing to land on both the Dean's academic and disciplinary lists.

And speaking of that Holy Trinity of sex, drugs, and rock 'n' roll, it wasn't long before I ventured off campus to attend my first "unofficial" soiree. Walking in the door, I was greeted by a flashing neon sign bearing the directive "Let's Fuck!" Funny—I'd read the standard articles warning of the difficulty of adjusting to college life, but somehow I wasn't feeling particularly homesick.

Like Palo Alto, Santa Barbara would never be confused with Selma or Birmingham in civil rights lore. However, in a college community during the 1960s, the issue could not be ignored completely. The growing but still miniscule number of minority students agitated for additional African American admissions and scholarships, courses relevant to race and ethnicity, and minority faculty hiring. My own energy was directed more toward protesting the American presence in Vietnam, but I did pitch in here and there to help out the brothers and sisters. In a classic example of youthful idealism and naivete, we circulated petitions to place the Peace and Freedom Party on the 1968 California presidential ballot. That effort was successful, but the nominee, Eldridge Cleaver—Black Panther leader, convicted felon, and a mere seven years shy of the constitutional age requirement for the presidency—somehow fell short of the White House.

As a student journalist, I interviewed many campus speakers, including civil rights activists. One gorgeous Friday afternoon, the sun sparkling off the ocean in the background as we contemplated the weekend's debauchery, fiery southern civil rights leader James Forman tried to refocus our attention. This was the first time I had ever heard the phrases "racist dog" and "fascist pig" uttered in the same sentence. Speaking with Forman afterward, he asked whether I had "gone South" during Freedom Summer in 1964. I doubt that my explanation that I was seventeen, just out of high school, and lacking parental permission was convincing. At the same event, I heard and interviewed Eduardo Mondlane, heroic commander of FRELIMO, the liberation forces of then-colonial Mozambique. In contrast to Forman's blunt, furious demeanor, Mondlane exhibited remarkable grace and patience. Alas, these qualities proved insufficient, as he was eventually assassinated.

I was among a group of students, including my future wife, a student of African history, who came under the tutelage of some charismatic faculty expatriates from South Africa, which was then in the brutal prime of apartheid. This hideous system of oppression, seemingly destined to end only in a tidal wave of blood, was often compared with our own brand of racial discrimination in those days. We demonstrated against American corporations doing business in South Africa, demanded the release of Nelson Mandela and other dissidents, and wrote letters to the President and Congress urging action. But apartheid remained strong; we had a lot to learn about patience and taking the long view.

The American anti-apartheid movement was in its infancy then, but it would gather great strength in the 1980s when I was in Washington. By that time, our numbers were gloriously greater as we demonstrated repeatedly at the South African Embassy. In the '90s, apartheid finally died at the negotiating table, not on the battlefield, and there were tears streaming down my face as I waved to a free and triumphant Mandela as he rode down Pennsylvania Avenue. As my family, teachers, supervisors, colleagues, and everyone else kept telling me: "Patience, patience."

⌇

During college summers, I worked briefly in dead-end (for the permanent working stiffs, but not for between-semesters Joe College) jobs back on the Peninsula, but I still felt the magnetic pull of the real world. This time, the compass pointed South. Twice, I embarked on the "Easy Rider" itinerary, from Texas to Florida, with similarly footloose and obligation-free friends, to witness the civil rights landscape firsthand and contribute our small part. In beat-up cars with California tags, sprouting long hair here and mustaches and beards there, we were off to God-knows-what end. We were the quintessential outsiders, direct from central casting—every southerner's nightmare come true.

I had read voraciously of the South—not just its unique history, but its literature. Its native writers—Warren, Styron, Faulkner, Ellison, O'Connor, Williams, Welty, Percy, Lee, Dickey, on and on—were my American favorites. Its roots music, absolutely central to my heart and soul, had always been nonpareil. It was the cradle not only of jazz, but of blues, rock 'n' roll, country, Cajun, Zydeco, rhythm & blues, gospel, everything I listened to and played. It was the sensual, kaleidoscopic landscape of my idol Chuck Berry's musical travelogues. But was also—in my simplistic worldview—the Land of Evil, where Neanderthal racists ran roughshod over helpless Negroes, a land to be punished for its grievous sins, if I had anything to say about it.

To say that these preconceptions—rather, prejudices—were based on limited first-hand knowledge would be a gross understatement. I had literally never set foot below the Mason-Dixon Line. I doubt whether I had ever knowingly held a conversation with a southerner. My most intimate contact with the South consisted of watching the Sugar, Cotton, and Orange Bowls on television on New Year's Day. It would be nice to report that my southern journeys resulted in a more even-handed understanding, empathy, or nuanced perspective. But I was a self-righteous, judgmental California teenager, whose moral universe did not allow for relativity or shades of gray. The undeniable dark side of the South flashed relentlessly across our television screens throughout the sixties, bomb after bomb, assassination after assassination, fire after fire. With a target this easy, why look closer to home for moral outrage?

My friends and I met, spoke to, and stayed with many southerners. We learned a lot: back then, not many southerners, black or white, were enjoying the prosperity we took for granted back in the Golden State; that college students, whatever their ethnicity, all have a vast amount of immaturity and hedonism to get out of their system; and that living in the midst of the civil rights revolution was a hell of a lot more complicated and challenging than watching it on television.

To our surprise, we ourselves were objects of considerable curiosity and amusement. During a stopover at a fraternity at Tulane University in New Orleans (we were desperate for cheap accommodations, just as I would be years later as a civil rights lawyer) we were the subject of a hastily convened "Meet the Press"-style interview with the alleged California Hippies. We were the anthropological highlight of everyone's summer. We were highly reliable sources of information on the sex and drug-soaked worlds of Haight-Ashbury, Sunset Strip, and other exotic California locales, and provided intimately-acquired details regarding film and rock stars. Our long-hair was the subject of constant laughter, scorn, and astonishment in diners and dormitories, as well as golf courses, monasteries, and other make-shift, no-cost sleeping quarters.

The generation gap, or counterculture rebellion, was just gathering steam in the South, and our white, often collegiate counterparts saw us as esteemed experts. They were hospitable and open. The draft loomed just as threateningly for them as for us, and we loved the same music. When the topic of race came up, most people let us know that they were sympathetic to the changes that were starting to seem inevitable. Who knows how much of this was for our consumption, but we encountered no apparent barn-burners.

Our black acquaintances and hosts were less forthcoming, understandably unsure where we were coming from and hardly conditioned to trust strange visitors. Once our proud liberal credentials became clear, our hosts opened up a bit, and we were graciously fed and housed, but few souls were bared. They'd been burned before, and just who the hell were we? Dilettante adventurers, who would be long-gone while their own life-long struggle for rights and respect continued on. This dynamic resurfaced for me in my Klan-busting days; I always had a ticket home tucked in my back pocket, but the locals would have to live with the consequences of my actions.

We visited many landmarks in the still-unfolding civil rights landscape. We giddily photographed each other next to the plaque honoring white supremacy at the Alabama state capital in Montgomery. We drove by, but of course didn't patronize, the Atlanta barbecue restaurant where Georgia governor-to-be Lester Maddox, distributed ax handles for the segregationist cause. We shot baskets in the gym at Texas Western University in El Paso, home of the newly-crowned first all-black team to win the NCAA basketball tournament; and viewed, wide-eyed, a steady stream of "White" and "Colored" signs not yet banished by the new civil rights laws. We had never seen these signs requiring separate dining rooms, drinking fountains, waiting rooms, recreation facilities, and the like. It was indeed an education.

Our only real trouble came—as it always does—on the back roads. Leaving the main highways to get a better glimpse of the Old South, we picked up hitchhikers, still a common practice in those less crime-ridden days. We didn't realize that the highways, too, were governed by the pervasive code of segregation. Whites picked up whites, and blacks took care of their own. When we pulled over to offer rides to black ride-seekers, we were met with amazement and reluctance. Finally, as we learned to be appropriately welcoming and assuring, some African-Americans accepted rides with us, but they slumped down below the level of the windows. This was just a local custom—it was a lesson learned from some horrific incidents that were triggered by the sight of racially-mixed automobile travel. We were also told that riding the back roads at all—let alone in racially mixed fashion—was foolhardy for black folks after dark. We had some fine conversations, learning what riders felt comfortable telling us about their own lives. We were strangers in a strange land, generally asking one too many questions. The rest was silence, broken only by the radio, Ray Charles or Johnny Cash singing of those very lonesome highways we were traveling.

Cruising through the back-country of Hancock County, Mississippi late one afternoon, we were suddenly cut off by a screeching, battered, and unmarked car. An aging fellow in civilian clothes, who gave no reason for stopping us even when asked, peppered us with questions regarding our destination, home-town, purpose of travel, local contacts, and vital statistics. Not satisfied with our responses, he collected our car keys, and, without a word, retreated to his vehicle for what seemed like an interminable length of time. This was clearly not a good sign, but we were just apprehensive, not yet afraid. After all, we are golden children from the Golden State. We knew people; we were untouchable.

Eventually with still no explanation forthcoming, we were driven deep into the woods to a small building with a Mississippi flag in front. By the time we were confined in a holding area, we were way past the "apprehensive stage'—it was cold sweat-time. I may have retained complete control over my bodily functions, but I wouldn't swear to it under oath. As we exchanged some nervous, inane remarks among ourselves (we were too naïve to understand the reason for our custodial status), we were told to shut up. Eventually, we were escorted into a primitive courtroom, where an even older gentleman, with one leg and a nasty stare, repeated the questions which the policeman (or whoever he was) had asked us on the highway. He gave us a hellacious lecture, along the lines of Californians having no legitimate purpose in these parts, and that we probably all deserved a good whipping (there goes that bodily function control again). We were ordered to pay—immediately, in cash—a fine, apparently for pissing off the local powers-that-be, and admonished to keep on moving eastward and out of Mississippi. Obeying this last directive would be no problem. Chastened and poorer, we redeemed our car in the parking lot, back on the road again.

Ever cocky and naive, we covered up our fright with false bravado, joking "Here come the judge," among other brilliant observations. That evening, safely across the border in the friendlier confines of Alabama, we casually related this tale to some new acquaintances. They didn't see the humor, reminding us that not long ago and not far away, civil rights workers James Chaney, Andrew Goodman, and Mickey Schwerner were apprehended under similar circumstances, never to draw another breath. We were informed that we weren't pulled over by accident—we were almost surely tracked by police or their informers once we entered the county, given our California tags and exotic appearance. We were deemed fools for driving on the back roads in the first place, and fools we were indeed.

We were likely fortunate that the explosion of publicity following the murders of Chaney, Goodman, and Schwerner, and similar incidents, had taught the local authorities that any more serious action directed against us could have caused more trouble than would have been worth their while. The Chaney, Goodman, and Schwerner killings, by a Ku Klux Klan contingent including law enforcement officers and clergy, had galvanized nationwide support for the civil rights movement. Sadly but undeniably, it had required the deaths of two young white men from the North for public outrage to reach a new level.

And that wasn't paranoia talking when we were told that we'd been scouted. When early threats to the colossus of segregation first appeared, Mississippi established and funded an official State Sovereignty Commission, complete with intelligence operatives and neighborhood spy networks, "to protect the sovereignty of the state from federal encroachment." I had not yet entered law school, but I'd thought that last issue had been settled at Appomattox in 1865.

Forty years after that southern journey, now a musician with the legal world fast fading in my rear-view mirror, I received a phone call, asking if I could play some piano blues for an art exhibit in Northern Virginia benefiting struggling artists from, of all places, Hancock County, recently devastated by Hurricane Katrina (the county had also been ravaged by Hurricane Camille in 1969). It turned out to be a delightful evening of funky music and down-home food and drink. I was told that back home, on the Mississippi Gulf Coast after the hurricane, local juke-joints, bands and arts cooperatives were increasingly integrated, and that residents, both black and white, were working together to resurrect the community. Things change.

With college graduation on the horizon, having been tantalized by a taste of the real world beyond California, it was once again time to do my Huck Finn thing and set out for new territory, this time Washington, D.C. I was impatient, easily bored, and stubbornly averse to taking the path of least resistance or doing what was expected of me. Law school seemed to make sense: it required no particular undergraduate major or skill set (God knows I had none!), and it suited my naive obsession with doing battle with the bad guys. As someone supposedly once said, you had to know the law to change it. Once more, I first appeared headed for UCLA, but, with the whim that marked most of my major life decisions, I opted instead for George Washington University in the nation's capital.

What the Hell, I thought; if I was going to play Don Quixote and change the world, why not go to the seat of power? I knew absolutely nothing of the law or law school. No one in my family had any legal experience or education. Indeed, I could locate only one person on either branch of the family tree who had ever come within a hundred miles of any type of college. I didn't know a soul in Washington. But I was a hopeless optimist, a true child of 1960s California: If it feels good, do it!

Stars in our eyes, my mercifully trusting wife of one year and I headed East, all our worldly goods crammed into her creaking Volkswagen bug, headin' down the highway, lookin' for adventure. And there was plenty of adventure, starting that first night, when we broke down on the eerie moonscape of the Bonneville Salt Flats in Utah, where howling coyotes far outnumbered any humans in the immediate vicinity. Four days later, we hit the capital of the free world in one piece (at least physically), fearless pilgrims utterly without a clue.

We needed a place to stay as soon as we arrived; both the Volkswagen and our funds were fast wearing thin. We found an apartment for rent across the Potomac in Arlington, Virginia, and prepared to check out these tiny but desperately-needed quarters. But it wasn't the apartment that was open for inspection—it was us. The property manager assured us that we were the appropriate shade for the landlord's color wheel, and provided us invaluable information on the location of nearby neighborhoods with high concentrations of "niggers." Congress had passed the Fair Housing Act—which I would later enforce—the previous year, but apparently it hadn't quite kicked in yet.

Many of the local streets, parks, and schools were named for presidents, but none for Lincoln. Unlike California, his birthday was not celebrated in the Old Dominion of Virginia. The sole Lincoln reference was to the most famous landmark in our lackluster neighborhood: the laundromat where American Nazi Party Führer George Lincoln Rockwell was assassinated (I would do battle with his crowd another day). The nearest restaurant, aptly named Whitey's, featured violent, sometimes fatal battles between the Pagans and the Saints, Northern Virginia's two most notorious biker gangs. The governor was a segregationist Democrat, soon to be succeeded by a racially-progressive Republican. This was a new world for us. We were now living in the northernmost part of the South, but we were still, as the locals put it, walking below The Line.

Law school proved to be basically unchanged from the crusty turn-of-the-century American model, featuring in-class humiliation of students and competition rather than cooperation. This atmosphere prepared us well for the legal culture at large. The male (naturally) faculty was a Whiter Shade of Pale, sporting gray suits and Ivy League class rings. While I can't deny that it prepared me adequately for law practice, I found it to be an interminable, numbingly-boring slog. There was almost no exposure to real cases or clients.

But for once, I followed everyone's advice and didn't challenge this musty system too aggressively; it was not yet ready for change, something one had to endure to become a practicing attorney. Graduate; pass the bar examination; then, feel free to slay all the dragons you wish. Sprinkled throughout our vast, Vietnam-era class was a tiny smattering of women and minorities. The former had a tough time in class at the hands of the all-powerful, traditionalist faculty, but they persevered. The black contingent did quite well academically, giving the lie to anti-affirmative action hysteria. I'd like to think that we the more privileged majority extended the support that these pioneers deserved—the memory fades.

To give credit where credit is due, there was an experimental class in civil rights law—this concept was so new that there was no standard casebook, just some mimeographed, stapled bits of court opinions and legislation. Other than the sporadic intrusion of tear gas into the classroom during anti-war demonstrations (we were, after all, in the nation's capital during the Age of Nixon), there was precious little contact with the real world.

During one droning first-year lecture, in a portent of things to come, a fellow piano man sitting next to me sagely remarked, "Man, this is bullshit." I couldn't disagree, but I had resolved to stick it out, and few could match me for sheer, mindless stubbornness. But this romantic soul, leading with his heart rather than his head, literally walked out the door, to resume a life previously spent in piano bars, nightclubs, and other shady venues. After a 25-year legal detour, I was right behind him.

I spent my early years at the bar with a succession of legal aid programs, struggling leftovers from Lyndon Johnson's War on Poverty. I represented the less fortunate in courtrooms, in the halls of Congress, and in ramshackle neighborhood offices. I traversed the mean streets of the riot-torn, poverty-stricken sections of the capital city that never appeared in the tourist guides, getting threatened and mugged for my trouble. I made plenty of rookie mistakes and tried to learn from them. I was pretty good at this stuff, but nothing special; I won a few, lost a few. And I wondered, more and more, whether a California free spirit like me was really cut out for the culture of the law, with all of its tradition and hierarchy, contentiousness and conceit.

Washington was a tense place in those days. The city had yet to recover, physically or emotionally, from the terrible 1968 riots in the wake of Martin Luther King's assassination. There were few remaining legal barriers to integration, but the capital was two worlds apart, black and white, warily eyeing—and suspecting the worst of—each other. Everyone seemed to be waiting for the other shoe to drop. One day, an envelope marked "United States Department of Justice" arrived in the mail. To my comrades and me back in the Golden State, this would have meant brushing up on Canadian geography or asking friends and relations for bail money, but that world was behind me. Inside the envelope, Deputy Attorney General Harold Tyler, former federal judge and lion of the establishment bar, welcomed me to the Civil Rights Division, warning that I was expected to put all else aside and "make a significant contribution to federal law enforcement."

I wasn't too sure about that, but I did recall that mysterious chart of racial injustice on my bedroom wall back on the Peninsula, with its unavenged lynchings and similar abominations. Apparently, all these many years later, I would have the opportunity to do battle with the very forces of evil that had always obsessed me. If ever a job existed with my name written all over it, this was it. I was about to turn thirty, when, according to classic '60s rhetoric, I was no longer to be trusted. I had no idea whether I was up to this challenge. But it was time to find out.

Fire on the Bayou

Hitler at the Post Office

It was a clear, sparkling southern morning in Willacoochee, Georgia. The inevitable heat and humidity had yet to kick in with their strength-sapping fierceness here on the outskirts of Savannah, that model of historic Old South preservation. My two companions and I exited the Southern Sportsman, where the men, and a few pioneering women, representing the fast-rising business class of the New South, gathered to sip coffee and trade news before heading out to make their fortunes. But we three, a most unlikely trio of musketeers, had a very different destination: the heart of South Georgia Ku Klux Klan country.

I was fairly new to the Justice Department Civil Rights Division's Criminal Section, having spent several years litigating civil cases involving school desegregation and housing discrimination. I had been in Savannah for two days planning this latest foray with Fitz Ormon Clarke, Jr., a diligent and very experienced FBI agent with a highly useful Dixie heritage and accent, as well as a wry sense of humor, not the most common trait in the standard Bureau catalogue. Clarke, a quietly confident southern gentleman and veteran of "Top Gun" Naval Aviation training, had few competitors when it came to law enforcement and civilian contacts throughout the state. And we would probably need just about all of them in the months ahead.

Earlier that morning we had picked up our final partner at the airport, Ricky Roberts, my Criminal Section colleague. At this point in our careers, Ricky was everything I was not in the Justice Department pecking order. An experienced criminal prosecutor, with several cases of considerable national importance behind him, he was Ivy League educated, well-connected politically, and very comfortable in the courtroom and on the road. He had graciously consented to serve as a veteran "second chair" on this challenging case. As an African-American about to serve a long tour of duty as far behind the lines as possible, he was likely to experience no small number of indignities beyond those which Clarke and would encounter. But like Clarke and myself, he worked for Mother Justice—this is what he had signed up for, and there would be no complaints.

Piling into Clarke's unglamorous FBI sedan, we made one final stop at the Bureau office in downtown Savannah, to gather up bulging briefcases and many boxes of documents. On this first day, we would drive 150 miles of rural Georgia highway—generally considered to be the nation's worst road system. We had to be sure to bring along everything we need, as we were effectively leaving civilization for the Third World. Each of us had been down these back roads before, but, as we would find out, never in quite so isolated and ominous a setting.

Cracking lame jokes to ease the tension—along the lines of Clarke and I denying any knowledge of our companion when the shit hit the fan, Roberts and I headed toward the parking lot, but Fitz was not quite ready. He punched in the combination to the secured door to the armory, where he checked out two shotguns, an extra pistol, and several boxes of shells and ammunition. "All right," he told us, flashing his best smile, "now we're ready to roll." Suddenly, Ricky and I were not so talkative. We looked at each other uncertainly, both likely thinking the same thing: We're not in Kansas anymore.

༄

> *From The New York Times:* WILLACOOCHEE, GA (AP)—*The Federal Bureau of Investigation says it will conduct a "preliminary inquiry" this week into a series of shootings, cross-burnings and threats aimed at racially mixed families in this rural southern Georgia county. Jim McMullen of the bureau's office in Savannah said Friday that agents would be sent to Atkinson County tomorrow to investigate the incidents, which began April 17 with a cross-burning in the front yard of Maureen Hood's home, where blacks and whites often played basketball together. Since then, according to the local authorities, shots have been fired into two homes, a shotgun has been fired at a parked car at the home of a white couple who have a black child, and threatening letters have been sent to more than 35 people, mostly blacks. A letter mailed July 19 said: "Attention Good Black People of Atkinson County. The Ku Klux*

> *Klan means you no harm. The danger is only to the race mixers who live in our midst."* Earl Haskins, the sheriff, said: *"I've never known there to be a Klan in this county, even in the '30s. I suspect it's some local people acting on their own and copying the Klan."*

༄

This article, one of several to appear in the national media, was basically accurate as far as it went, but it did not begin to show the extent of the climate of fear that Klan activity had spread throughout Atkinson County. In addition, as we would learn, the good sheriff was lying through his teeth. But that would all surface later. By the morning of our initial drive from Savannah, I had already written my "prosecutive summary," the standard Justice Department memorandum recommending grand jury investigation, with a detailed analysis of strengths, weaknesses, evidence to date, and preliminary plan of attack. John Lee Maynes, up-and-coming Georgia KKK leader, had been identified through FBI fingerprint and typewriter analysis as the author of the threatening letters, with further evidence to be developed through the federal grand jury process.

Like all but one of the prosecutive summaries I drafted during my time in the Criminal Section, this one was approved by my supervisors, who would also have to ratify any subsequent decision to seek an indictment. My lone rejection had come several months earlier in a case involving a black homeowner in a previously all-white Chicago neighborhood, who had been plagued by continuous harassment. He finally surprised a group of rock-throwing tormentors, wounding them, although not seriously, with a shotgun blast as they fled. At the behest of the U.S. Attorney's Office in Chicago—a powerful unit within the Justice Department hierarchy—my recommendation to prosecute the neighborhood youths was overruled, on grounds that we could appear to be condoning vigilante justice. Other than this matter, I had received the full support of my superiors.

The Atkinson County Klan campaign was my first major Ku Klux Klan case, so on my way to Savannah I stopped in Atlanta for some expert advice (in those days, one had to fly through Atlanta to reach most southern destinations anyway; thus the standard phrase "see you in Atlanta" that was so often exchanged between civil rights attorneys). I was fortunate to meet with Robert Ensley of Justice's Community Relations Services, an office specializing in defusing dangerous racial hostilities. Ensley, an African American veteran of some truly hellacious confrontations throughout the South, gave me the basic lay of the land for Atkinson County, a jurisdiction so far off the beaten track that even most Georgians had never heard of it. Sensing my relative newness to this milieu, he generously offered advice on survival, figuratively and literally. He spoke of clandestine alliances; unspoken family and community ties; poor, struggling people, both black and white, who trusted no one, particularly outsiders; and the certainty that the locals would know my movements no matter what precautions I took. Looking back on this meeting of the wise and the innocent, I'm sure that Ensley was thinking something like, "Son, you might as well be wearing a New York Yankees cap down there."

When a community is in the grip of a Ku Klux Klan reign of terror, you don't just know it intellectually; you experience it physically. The ions in the atmosphere crackle with fear, uncertainty, and suspicion. The heat and humidity are even more oppressive than usual, draining you of initiative and resourcefulness. Night seems to fall earlier; the sunrise takes a bit longer to pierce the gloom. The clouds hang lower, and the horizon is nearer; there is less room to maneuver. Greetings are more perfunctory.

People meeting in the street don't linger quite as long. Conversations are hushed, or whispered. There is little banter or laughter. Telephone conversation is less candid. And towards the end of the day, unfinished business is hastily concluded. Best not to be out at night, when demons, known and unknown, run free.

⁌

"Welcome to Atkinson County, motherfucker. Enjoy your trip, 'cause it might be your last."

That was the telephone greeting I received shortly after we checked in to our motel in neighboring Coffee County (Atkinson having no hostelries). Not particularly inventive as such welcomes go, but not exactly soothing to the nerves. Mentioning this to special agent Clarke (who had received similar messages from Maynes himself), he reminded me never to use my real name in hotel registers. That night, we slept on mattresses on the floor, and thereafter we made sure that the shades were pulled down at all times, day and night. Clarke, ever the relaxed, confident professional, laughed and feigned surprise that the motel manager might have tipped off our targets as to our location. Get used to it, Howard, I told myself; never let them see you sweat.

The town of Willacoochee was and is about what its name sounds like. With a population of 1,400, in a county whose total was just 6,000, one-third African American—it was truly near no people, places, or things of any prominence. It was the type of community in which not only did everyone know everyone else and their business, but many residents were also related. There were not all that many last names in the phone book. When our travels took us to larger towns such as Brunswick and Waycross for pretrial hearings and grand jury sessions, they seemed like Atlanta or Chicago by comparison. We trudged through countless peach farms, melon groves, lumber mills, and other sweltering, sometimes rain-soaked, outdoor venues, in search of any lead or clue. Our indoor discussions took place overwhelmingly in various auto repair businesses, a favorite Klan place of employment. To this day, many of my dreams—rather, nightmares —play out in the suffocating atmosphere of Baby Jesus Brake and Transmission Service, a huge confederate battle-flag always nailed to the wall.

We were relentless in our pursuit of any information which might tighten the noose around Maynes, our chief target. Clarke put out the word, through his local law enforcement contacts, that anyone with admissible evidence against Maynes would be a prime candidate for lenient treatment, and the sooner they cooperated with us, the better things would go for them. While our fingerprint and typewriter evidence seemed rock solid—and certainly there was little doubt as to Maynes' racial views—we would likely need corroborating witnesses to convince twelve jurors of his guilt beyond a reasonable doubt. But we were not just dealing with a close-knit community hostile to outsiders; we were up against a Ku Klux Klan wall of silence every bit as strict as organized crime's code of *omerta*.

We did gather additional bits of physical evidence here and there. At our first grand jury session, our leadoff witness was a young, strikingly attractive female F.B.I. agent, one of the nation's first. She was able to establish a solid, although not infallible, connection between the cross burned on Maureen Hood's lawn and wood and fastening materials taken from Maynes's property. The sight of this pioneering agent, her short orange dress riding up on her frame while she struggled to carry an eight-foot tall, charred and flaking sacred religious symbol, formed a hideously twisted, almost pornographic image of our entire mission into the depravity of the hate-maddened human mind. Good God, I wondered: what in the world was I doing here?

Our relations with local law enforcement yielded precious little in the way of cooperation. Marion "Lace" Futch, the recently-elected mayor of Willacoochee, was reasonably bright and affable. But he had demonstrated sympathy for Concerned Citizens of Atkinson County, a predominantly black organization formed to protest the Klan activity. As a new member of the power structure, he was suspect anyway, and this show of support for an upstart group cut him off from the KKK-law enforcement-business ruling coalition and their intelligence network. And there was one additional problem: Futch was a convicted felon, having served time in federal prison for theft of government property. This was not exactly what we wanted a jury to hear about our most promising witness.

We suspected that the longtime county sheriff, Earl Haskins, knew a whole lot more than he let on, either to the New York Times or to us. He could never quite look us in the eye, and we presumed that he was warning others not to be too forthcoming with we three musketeers from Washington. A sheriff in a rural Deep South county back in the day was more monarch than mere elected official, and you didn't cross him if you knew what was good for you.

Furthermore, as we later found out, he had his own criminal enterprises to protect from outside intervention. Haskins' ally, Hal Baxley, whom Maynes had unsuccessfully asked Futch to appoint as Willacoochee police chief, was believed by many to be the local KKK Klavern leader, now that Maynes had ascended to statewide leadership. But, once again, we could not break through the wall of silence to prove it.

In Atkinson County there was plenty of what passed for local color. You just had to see it that way, and try to laugh to keep from crying. Willacoochee policeman Ross Davis served as the designated "good cop," a counterweight to his passive-aggressive confederates; he was always ready with a joke or a cup of coffee. One afternoon, noting my admiration for an orange, tiger-logo "Willacoochee" T-shirt that a passer-by was wearing, he urged me to go into the general store and "see if you can Jew 'em down on the price of one of those shirts." I was tempted to react, but you had to pick your battles selectively on official travel and keep your eyes on the prize. Realistically, I was probably not a leading candidate to bring political correctness to these parts. I purchased the shirt, but I paid retail.

This was just one of many observations on my exotic religious heritage. The wife of Maynes's defense attorney, like many other locals, delighted in pronouncing my name in a variety of innovative ways. "My, my, Mr. Fahn-stern, how evah do you pronounce your name," she loved to exclaim. But I was there to enforce federal law, not my own delicate sensibilities. Grin and bear it brother, I would tell myself—you're way below the line.

But some insults are worse than others. Early on in our journey, we noticed that Maynes, a wild-eyed, massively-built, and imposing figure with unruly hair, mustache, and flowing beard, was often referred to as the "liberal" in the family. That was because his wife, Willacoochee's postmistress, was a confirmed Nazi. Under our sacred First Amendment protections, she was certainly entitled to her views. However, nothing—not even advance warning from local officials—prepared me for the shock of seeing Adolf Hitler's portrait adorning the walls of the United States Post Office. I brought this to my section chief's attention in a phone call that evening. He reminded me, correctly, that none of us were down there as invited guests, and that I needed to concentrate on the task at hand. Predictably, this hilarious tale of rookie prosecutor Feinstein journeying through the Nuremberg South quickly made the rounds of the Criminal Section.

There was only one place to eat in Willacoochee. Every lunch-hour, at the entrance of the celebrity salt-and-pepper duo—Roberts, six-feet-six plus, rail-thin, plus prominent Afro, and the exotic Hebrew—the diner's regulars ceased conversation to gawk in silence. But at least those grand entrances were expected. One afternoon at the Willacoochee police station, Roberts and I walked in just as one officer's racial joke reached the critical punch-line. As he saw Ricky enter, the befuddled law enforcement officer stammered out a quickly improvised alternate ending to this tale, fondly recalled to this day by Fitz Clarke: "...so then he says, 'It must have been a n-n-n-n-, uh, colored guy.'"

And Ricky, possessed of an inner peace and easy adaptability that I would likely never attain, warmly greeted his fellow enforcers of the law and joined in the laughter.

Try as we might, day after sweltering day in the fields and storefronts, night after exhausting night comparing notes and combing through documents in our third-rate motel, we never really penetrated the hometown fortress of solidarity against outside inquiry. This being the South, football season eventually rolled around, and everyone was crazy over those Georgia Bulldogs, led by the All-American African American running back and Georgia native Herschel Walker. But precious few folks would lift a finger to help enforce the laws which gave Walker's brethren the fundamental rights due every American citizen, regardless of race, creed, or color. It was time to press on and ask the grand jury for an indictment based on what evidence we had managed to unearth to date, and then roll the dice at trial.

⁓

The preliminary grand jury sessions went smoothly, as Roberts and I introduced ourselves and explained the federal criminal civil rights laws to the 23 grand jurors, who met off and on for an eighteen-month term, based in Savannah, to decide whether probable cause existed to issue federal indictments. Special Agent Clarke then summarized, for the panel of his fellow Georgians, the Ku Klux Klan reign of terror and intimidation, and the evidence linking John Lee Maynes to the conspiracy. He was followed by our F.B.I. fingerprint expert from Washington, who tied Maynes to the various threatening letters. So much for the easy part.

After considerable blood, sweat, and tears, we were able to gain the cooperation of the identified victims of the Klan terror campaign before the grand jury—and ultimately at trial. This took no small amount of courage on the part of the witnesses. No matter how much support and protection against retaliation we could offer, these brave souls still had to live in Willacoochee, where personal safety and gainful employment were anything but secure. Federal grand jury investigations are secret proceedings, but as we had already learned, nothing stayed private for long in this neck of the woods. As always, we could not over-promise. Not everyone can enter the witness protection program, and the Department of Justice granted no lifetime guarantees. The grand jurors understood this as well, and remained riveted during the victims' accounts:

Maureen Hood was Maynes's next-door neighbor, who tutored local students, both white and black, and allowed her yard to be used for after-school recreation by these same children. She was our most confident witness, determined to do the right thing. Her lawn had been the site of the burnt cross previously viewed by the grand jury; the next morning, she had also discovered a white towel on her doorstep, emblazoned with the "KKK" logo. For good measure, she shortly thereafter received the same letter—on Ku Klux Klan stationery—sent to many other victims of the hate-spree:

The first visit was a warning. The second will be for real. LEAVE THIS COUNTY.

Finally, Hood testified that police officer Baxley—rumored to be head of the local KKK Klavern—had told her not to report any of these incidents. This not only put the grand jury on notice of the extent of the conspiracy of silence, but also answered any lingering questions as to why we interlopers from Washington were here, instead of leaving the situation to the local authorities.

Next was Earl Mabry, a struggling white tenant farmer, who was known to have a granddaughter of African American heritage. His house and pickup truck had been blasted by nighttime shotgun fire. He had later received the same "follow-up" letter as Maureen Hood.

Wynn Roy Burroughs was Mabry's landlord. He told the grand jury that he was uncertain what to do following the shooting on his property. However, he had no choice but to evict Mabry after being "scared shitless" soon afterward by the following letter:

Knights of the Ku Klux Klan

Dear Mr. Burroughs:

> I understand that you have a combination of niggers and white trash living in one of your tenant houses. I think that it would be in your best interest to let them know that they are not welcome anymore. I understand that the farming business contains enough bad luck without you having to worry about unnecessary bad luck. May our Lord, God, Persevere.

Sincerely yours,

Office of the Exalted Cyclops, South Georgia Klavern of the Invisible Empire, Knights of the Ku Klux Klan

Jack Slaughter was another victim of Maynes's perverse genealogical research; Slaughter was also rumored to have a black granddaughter. He had to endure the humiliating, but unfortunately necessary, ordeal of reading aloud to the grand jurors the letter he had received:

Knights of the Ku Klux Klan

Dear Mr. Slaughter:

I can't tell you anything that you don't already know. But perhaps I can make it plainer to you. Your daughter has brought shame and disgrace to you, her husband, herself, and to her family. This can not be changed. However, further suffering can be avoided. Why don't you disown the nigger loving whore as other fathers have done? Why take her in under your wing as you have done? Further protecting of her will only bring further suffering to your family as a whole. Think what your own family is saying behind your back.

"*If she was mine. I know what I'd do.*"

"*She likes a long black dick don't she.*"

"*Why don't she move to the nigger quarters with the bucks that's where she wants to be.*"

"*A white man just can't satisfy her.*"

May the Lord, God, Persevere.

Sincerely yours,

Office of the Exalted Cyclops, South Georgia Klavern of the Invisible Empire, Knights of the Ku Klux Klan

By this point in the proceedings, Roberts and I could barely stand to look at each other, let alone at the grand jurors. Commandeering this hideous testimony, I felt like some sick strain of pornographer. But we absolutely had to get this detailed history into the record before trial, and the grand jurors needed to understand the cumulative seriousness of the situation. Slaughter went on to relate that his tenant, C.R. Mathews (rumored to be his granddaughter's father), had his car shot up in the same manner and time as Mabry. Mathews had also been yet another recipient of the "LEAVE THIS COUNTY" message.

Will Comstock was an African-American mill worker with a family to support, and although Comstock had a lot to lose, he never flinched from telling the whole truth, in the grand jury or at trial. The midnight shotgun barrage fired into his tiny home barely missed his wife (who was white) and mother (who was black), and the shells matched those used in the other attacks. In addition to a copy of the "LEAVE THIS COUNTY" letter, with which the grand jurors by now were quite familiar, members of the Comstock family were recipients of the following communication, distributed to many black Atkinson County residents:

ATTENTION!
GOOD BLACK PEOPLE OF ATKINSON COUNTY

THE KU KLUX KLAN MEANS YOU NO HARM. THE KLAN IS DANGEROUS ONLY TO THE RACE MIXERS WHO LIVE IN OUR MIDST. WE REGRET THAT YOU HAVE FOUND IT NECESSARY TO SIGN THIS PIECE OF TOILET PAPER CALLED A RESOLUTION THAT THE RACE MIXERS HAVE FORCED UPON YOU. HOWEVER, YOUR SIGNATURE INDICATES THAT YOU SUPPORT RACE MIXING. WE ARE SURE YOU, THE GOOD BLACK PEOPLE WERE LED INTO

THIS BY THE JEW BACKED NAACP OR AS IT IS LOCALLY KNOWN THE WILLACOOCHEE ACTION COMMITTEE. THESE RACE MIXING WHITE TRASH AND BLACKS WILL CAUSE UNDUE SUFFERING TO INNOCENT BLACKS. GOOD BLACK PEOPLE YOU CAN STILL DISOWN THIS RACE MIXING TRASH WHILE THERE IS STILL TIME. THE ONLY REASON THEY ASKED YOUR HELP IS TO BRING YOU INTO THE DEPTHS OF HELL WHERE THEY ALREADY RESIDE. WE STAND BEFORE YOU TODAY TO CONTEND THAT WE HAVE ENOUGH RED BLOODED PROTESTANT AMERICAN CITIZENS TO SWEAR WITH THEIR HAND RAISED TO HEAVEN THAT WE WILL RIDE OUR HORSES IN BLOOD UNTIL THEIR BRIDLES FLOAT BEFORE WE WILL SUBMIT TO THIS RACE MIXING TRASH.

KU KLUX KLAN

Desperate for any excuse to relieve the tension we were experiencing day after day, we three Feds had a fine old time lampooning this piece of scholarship that evening back at our motel, with Fitz playing the red-blooded, All-American southern Protestant; yours truly as the crafty Jew behind the scenes, controlling the NAACP; and Ricky as one of the county's easily-duped "good black people." But in front of the grand jury, you could have heard a pin drop as Will Comstock matter-of-factly read aloud this missive from hell. And why shouldn't he have been stoic? It wasn't as though he hadn't heard it all before.

The final witness in this sad litany was Clement McMichaels, testifying to illustrate the utter insanity and recklessness of this reign of fear. A lumberman erroneously presumed to own the house in which Will Comstock and his family resided, McMichaels nonetheless had received copies of both the "LEAVE THIS COUNTY" letter and the "BRIDLES FLOATING IN BLOOD" decree. Our unstated, none-too-subtle message to the grand jury was: whether you be "race-mixing trash," a "good black citizen," or a confirmed segregationist, no one was immune from this kind of state of siege. It could happen to you.

There were plenty of additional witnesses we could have subpoenaed, but if the grand jury hadn't gotten the picture by now we were in serious trouble. We didn't want to wear out our welcome at that stage, and it was always best to hold an ace in the hole or two for trial. Fitz Clarke wound it all up with a crisply-delivered but comprehensive summary of the evidence, and all twenty-three citizens, tried-and-true, swiftly returned a five-count civil rights conspiracy indictment. Now came the hard part: the ordeal of trial where Maynes, ably assisted by counsel, could call his own witnesses and cross-examine ours. And there was no doubt about it: he'd be playing on his home field.

At the pretrial hearings, John Lee Maynes was a new man: clean-shaven; clad in suit and tie in place of country overalls, and speaking only when spoken to. This transformation, no doubt, came on orders from his new lawyer, Ted Solomon, an experienced South Georgia defense attorney. Maynes's fate would be decided by the usual all-white jury, as few African Americans in the South had yet joined the voter rolls from which federal jurors are summoned. The Voting Rights Act might have finally passed, but its enforcement would not come quickly.

There was one factor that we realized might be in our favor. Presiding over the trial in Waycross—near the Okefenokee Swamp on the Florida border, but a veritable metropolis after months in Atkinson County—would be the Honorable Anthony Alaimo. Originally from

Up North, Judge Alaimo enjoyed a long-standing reputation for diligence and fearlessness. The latter was well-earned: he had been a leader of a band of American servicemen who escaped from a German prison camp during World War II, subsequently immortalized in the 1963 film "The Great Escape," starring Steve McQueen. At least we knew there would be one person in the courtroom who would likely not be intimidated by the Ku Klux Klan.

But I was destined never to see that courtroom. A week before trial, I was laid low by the first in a maddening series of maladies that would eventually dispatch me back to the less dramatic precincts of civil rights enforcement. This time, it was a puzzling, extremely painful infection which my doctor believed may have been the result of many months in an unhygienic backwoods environment, drinking poorly treated water and being exposed to a myriad of other health hazards. I desperately resolved to make it to Waycross for trial, but several days before the start of jury selection, I was weak, burning with fever, and in considerable pain. Like an athlete relegated to the disabled list against his will, I was replaced by another attorney. Never have I felt so impotent, and I was insufferable—as my wife can still attest—in my self-pity.

Viewing the matter objectively, the lead prosecution chair could hardly have been in more capable hands than those of Ricky Roberts. Like me, he had lived with this case for what seemed like forever. Having been driven crazy on numerous occasions by phone calls from Washington while under pressure on the road, I resisted the temptation to call Ricky or Fitz for progress reports. They had enough on their plates.

At the end of the week, back in my office in a weakened condition, my phone rang. It was Ricky on the line, his voice reflecting no more or less emotion than usual:

"Not guilty on all counts."

And there was nothing, absolutely nothing, that I could say. As a Criminal Section colleague once told me following an identical verdict in an even larger Ku Klux Klan prosecution:

"It's like a death in the family."

⁓

I soon regained my health—at least temporarily. Everyone told me this would pass, and the thing to do was to plunge into some fresh cases—and that's what I did. But the unpunished Atkinson County Ku Klux Klan rampage did not pass for me, and it still hasn't. These things never do.

Ricky Roberts enjoyed considerable success in the Washington legal community, eventually becoming chief of the Civil Rights Division's Criminal Section. He is now a United States District Judge for the District of Columbia. Fitz Ormon Clarke, Jr. is retired from the F.B.I., enjoying life with his family on the South Georgia seacoast. Judge Alaimo, whom I was told gave the prosecution a fair deal at trial, served as a senior district judge until his death at 89. But Atkinson County Sheriff Earl Haskins—the man who could never look us in the eye—fell hard. In 1992 he was charged with providing protection to drug-dealers; cultivating a marijuana farm; and staging illegal cockfights, all for substantial personal profit. While awaiting trial, he hanged himself in his own jail.

By far the most unforeseeable post-trial path was that of the defendant, John Lee Maynes. Not long after his acquittal, he embarked upon on a course of higher education, culminating in a law degree. He hung out his shingle in neighboring Coffee County. But that is not the biggest surprise from our target. He published a notice, thanking "all the minority clients who have supported Mr. Maynes' law practice by using him as their lawyer." And then, John Lee Maynes, living symbol of everything we were pledged to engage in mortal combat, established a scholarship fund for minority college students from Atkinson and Coffee Counties.

⁓

Back at the office, Ricky and I rarely spoke of our time in South Georgia. What was done was done; we were busy young lawyers with careers to pursue, and our duties generally found us in different locations. But one day, I decided to bring up a piece of unfinished business that I couldn't seem to let go of. Ricky knew what it was before I could get the words out of my mouth. Together, we walked into the office of our section chief, Dan Rinzel. Agreeing that there was no downside to our request at this point, Rinzel gave us permission to inform the United States Post Office, on official Justice Department stationery, that they might wish to know that one of their Georgia outposts proudly displayed a photograph of Der Führer. We never did receive a reply.

All-American City

> *"I was standing there in the middle of [Chicago's] Gage Park when there was just a rain of rocks and cherry bombs. I was standing right next to Dr. King when he was hit. The violence in the South always came from a rabble element. But these were women and children and husbands and wives coming out of their homes becoming a mob—and in some ways it was far more frightening."*
>
> Andrew Young

There wasn't much for a bunch of teenage boys to do on a late August evening in the 1970s in South Williamsport, Pennsylvania, the bluest of blue-collar towns, deep in the mountains of north-central Pennsylvania. All local sources of amusement and novelty had long been exhausted. Most of these kids would soon begin, or resume, whatever dead-end employment still existed in the area. For some, summer jobs were ending, and it would be back to high school. A few were headed to vocational schools or community colleges, and a couple would be joining the Army, which offered security, housing, and food. One evening, the group—their lives at their peak, although they didn't realize it—gathered as usual on a grassy slope in an otherwise empty park, to drink beer and engage in whatever forms of obnoxious mischief came to mind.

Across Main Street, in a tiny, weather-worn house, lived Denise Bishop, thirty year-old single mother, with her son of nine, Carl. They had been in town barely a year, still new faces in a neighborhood where not many people left or moved in. Being African-American, the Bishop family was even more of a novelty, but the welcome wagon did not stop at their address. They had been a convenient, regular target for the boys on the hill, who had spent much of the summer hurling epithets at Mrs. Bishop, as well as rocks at the family cat and beer cans at her car.

One night, Denise Bishop's imperturbable restraint finally cracked, and she yelled at the crew to leave her alone and get the hell out of there. The battle was joined. Once more, Denise Bishop heard the same old take on her ancestry, skin color, chastity, and general unsuitability for residence in the All-American city. Running out of beer and fresh insults, the boys eventually scattered, on to the next engagement in the evening's battle with boredom. But one of them had a better idea.

Jon Berofsky, not quite eighteen but rough and ready after another beer or two, proceeded to a nearby lumber yard; helped himself to some scrap wood; and constructed a five-foot tall cross. It was a quick trip back to the Bishops residence, where he pounded the cross into the lawn and sets it ablaze, ten feet from the front window. To make sure that his craftsmanship did not go unnoticed, Berofsky unleashed a barrage of rocks against the little house's aluminum siding, awakening first Carl, and then his mother. Tires screeching, Jon made haste to rendezvous with his buddies, now armed with a tale that would be hard to top for that evening.

"Momma! Momma! What's that?" asked Carl, in a fiery netherworld between dream and reality. Denise, fiercely hugging her child and trying to keep it together, had never witnessed this scene before, but she recognized it for precisely what it was. In fact, she had recently been wondering if it might be time to have The Conversation with her son, the same one her mother had long ago with her—indeed, the same one all black parents must eventually hold with their children, to explain, and psychologically arm them against, man's inhumanity to man. She just never realized that it would be that soon, under those circumstances. God help the child.

~

One year later, a slim file folder summarizing these events appeared amidst the clutter of my desk. That's how it always started. Before the fireworks, before the headlines, before the tears, there were reports to read, notes to take, and memoranda to draft. Well before any case turned to flesh and blood, it had to successfully navigate the bureaucratically daunting paper trail of the United States Department of Justice. Whenever a citizen made an initial complaint alleging a federal civil rights violation, it was reviewed at the local FBI field office; by the Civil Rights Unit at FBI headquarters in Washington; and by a paralegal in the Justice Department Civil Rights Division's Criminal Section. If the line attorney (yours truly, in the Bishop case) proposed presenting the matter to a federal grand jury, it needed the approval of the Criminal Section's Deputy and Chief. Next, the opinion of the local United States Attorney's office was obtained. Finally, the Assistant Attorney General for Civil Rights had to approve going forward. In cases of particular notoriety or sensitivity, the matter would be referred to the Attorney General's office as well.

There were many potential obstacles along this path. The matter might not involve federal law at all ("That damn kid keeps delivering my newspaper in the bushes instead of on the front porch."). There might be insufficient injury or other personal detriment to warrant a jury's attention or sympathy ("Just because I called him a motherfucking pig, the cop put the handcuffs on me too tight."). The First Amendment's broad reach barred many prosecutions, often in sympathetic situations (Ku Klux Klan or Nazi party rallies in minority neighborhoods; racist diatribes on radio or television). Sometimes, specific defendants were not clearly identified. The technological advances have improved this situation significantly, but it was very difficult in my day to get fingerprints from rough wooden crosses, not to mention DNA evidence from sexual or physical assaults. And very often, because criminal prosecutors must convince a unanimous jury of guilt beyond a reasonable doubt, there was just not enough evidence to go forward. This could be heartbreaking when we had no doubt that a victim of racial intimidation or police brutality was telling the truth, but without neutral eye-witnesses or solid physical evidence, we had only a slim chance of prevailing against a half-way decent defense attorney.

My Civil Rights Division school desegregation and Ku Klux Klan cases were always in the South. But ugly episodes like the Bishop case occurred everywhere. The North had always been just as resistant—if not more so—to the integration of all-white neighborhoods as the South. This case was somewhat controversial, as it had previously been recommended for closing by the United States Attorney's Office in Pennsylvania, as well as by another Criminal Section attorney (no longer with the office). But our Deputy Chief, Linda Davis, wasn't quite ready to abandon ship; fairly new to the section and to the world of criminal law, I was assigned to take another look.

The major reasons for the previous declinations were the fact that Berofsky and his companions were legally juveniles at the time of the incident; Berofsky had no prior criminal record or Ku Klux Klan-type affiliation; and the incident was characterized as a youthful prank by both the town police and the local FBI office. I could imagine their line of thinking: there might well be a technical violation of federal civil rights law, but let's not make a federal case out of it. On the other hand, Denise Bishop had a spotless record; Berofsky had at no time expressed any remorse; and the victim still wanted justice, despite being told by the local police: "This is no big deal. Don't worry about it."

Berofsky had admitted his actions, after being apprehended in short order by the local police, but the Lycoming County District Attorney swiftly declined prosecution. Weighing all of these factors, I decided to draft a detailed prosecutive summary, recommending that we go forward.

Discussing the case with Deputy Chief Davis was, as always, an experience. It brought back memories of merciless cross-examination by cruel professors during the first year of law school. Although she was responsible for many more cases than me, she knew the details of this one better than I did. How does she do it? I wondered, as she grilled me on the case's strengths and weaknesses, evidentiary issues, the backgrounds of everyone involved, potential prosecution and defense witnesses, and God knows what else. Of particular concern was the impossibility of the usual grand jury investigation, which was not permitted in federal juvenile matters. This meant that I would be unable to assess the credibility and persuasiveness of potential witnesses under oath, nor have the critical opportunity to subpoena evidence. Accordingly, I was instructed to spend whatever time it would take in Williamsport to thoroughly interview the entire cast of characters, and to become intimately familiar with every fact and figure of this case. There were to be no surprises at trial. If this meant intruding on the traditional investigative turf of the FBI—who had not been enthusiastic about pursuing this matter—then that would be their problem.

By this time, I should have expected no less from Davis. Like her colleagues in Criminal Section management, she combined the typical prosecutor's adversary nature with an intimidating demeanor. She would hear no excuses, and no question was ever to be answered with the pathetic phrase "I don't know." She possessed in abundance—and expected from each of us—the "fire in the belly" to do whatever it took, obstacles be damned, to win these cases.

I didn't understand it back then, but she was the type of supervisor, mentor, tormentor—however you might phrase it—who ultimately could make you into the type of prosecutor you needed to be in order to win cases as challenging as ours. But that didn't mean I had to enjoy the process. I dreaded being summoned into my supervisors' offices—it was never a pleasant experience. Seated on the other side of their massive desks, my own chair always lower, I was always tempted to ask that I be read my rights before the interrogation began. Ask any prosecutor, and you'll hear a similar description. The office soundtrack features "I Won't Back Down," not "Kumbaya."

Davis' relentless pursuit of justice in her own investigations and prosecutions was legendary, rocketing her to supervisory status in record time on an overwhelmingly male, testosterone-intensive playing field. My first Criminal Section assignment, a year or so earlier, had been to research potential legal theories for a factually compelling, but legally tenuous, prosecution. I was amazed to review a previous case file in which Davis, then very new to the Criminal Section, had pressed on to the highest levels of the Justice Department, over repeated rejections, in support of an utterly novel theory for a particularly horrific crime.

She simply would not take no for an answer. We had our clashes over the years, and I certainly can't say I ever looked forward to being called into her office. Like her management colleagues, whatever praise she afforded us was rare and grudging. The enforcement of civil rights law was viewed as a holy mission, which we were privileged to be involved in—nothing to be thanked or complimented.

But when we were on the road, naked and alone before a formidable array of unfamiliar adversaries, our bosses had our backs. Whenever a clash erupted with the FBI, a U.S. Attorney, a judge, or any number of our various tormentors—and I seemed to specialize in those—we had the full support of the front office. They had all been down that road before, and they never asked us to do anything they hadn't done themselves many times.

The U.S. Attorney's office remained unenthusiastic, but they didn't object to our prosecuting Berofsky, as long as it was understood that the ball was in our court. Fair enough. I arranged to head up to Williamsport as soon as possible to get the lay of the land; I cleared my docket and coordinated schedules with the FBI assigned to the case. I was ready to roll, but first, there was one more item to take care of. I placed a call to Denise Bishop, who had since moved across the Susquehanna River to Williamsport proper, in search of some peace and quiet. I introduced myself; informed her that the Department of Justice would be pursuing her case; and that I'd be up to meet with her next week. There was a quick intake of breath on the line, followed by a long pause. Then:

"You're from the United States Justice Department? You mean to tell me that you're coming up here from Washington, D.C. for my case? I can't believe it! I can't believe it!"

A little of that went a long way. In my world, gratitude was rare indeed. Denise Bishop's reaction upon learning that the federal government had decided to intervene on her behalf case was very gratifying. On the other hand: what a sad commentary that this recognition of her clear rights under the Constitution and federal law should evoke such surprise, and that I should be thanked for being magnanimous when I was simply doing my job.

∽

In the fading light of a late autumn afternoon, I grabbed a cab to the Washington Navy Yard, in a desolate section of the capital, and checked out my official General Services Administration car, courtesy of Uncle Sam. This drab, bare-bones hulk, all but screaming "government issue," would surely announce my presence to anyone in Williamsport who didn't already know I was in town. It was a distinctly unscenic five-hour drive, winding past such depressing landmarks as Three Mile Island, site of America's closest brush with nuclear disaster, and the twin delights of Allenwood and Lewisburg Federal Prisons. The latter was referred to in the local U.S. Attorney's Office as "our 2000-student law school, where no innocent man dwells." The only city en route was Harrisburg, which would seem just as lackluster ugly thirty years later, when I performed there at a blues festival, in a park which had to be cleared by 10:00 p.m., due to the unsafe nature of the neighborhood.

It was pitch dark when I arrived in Williamsport, and a frigid wind howled down from the mountain passes. I tried a restaurant recommended by a paralegal from another Civil Rights Division section. It was old, mildewed, and drafty. The food was reminiscent of high school cafeterias. Was it my imagination, or was I always up North in the cold months and baking down South during summer?

I took a quick look around town early next morning. The Little League World Series was finished for the year, but red-white-and-blue bunting and streamers were everywhere, proclaiming the All-American virtues of the community. But this was not prosperous country. The houses were small and bare; old-style country music wailed mournfully on the radio, and the roads were full of pick-up trucks and cars well past their prime. School was closed for the opening day of deer season. This was big-time hunting country, and the coffee shops were abuzz with sportsmen heading out for the mountains. The one thing that didn't seem to fit was the "James Brown Public Library"—something tells me it was named for someone other than the Godfather of Soul. I was reminded of James Carville's classic description: Pennsylvania is Philadelphia to the east, Pittsburgh to the west, and Alabama in the middle. I couldn't have been more alien if I'd just alighted from a spaceship.

My first appointment was at a diner with FBI Special Agent Craig Reese. It was always critical to establish rapport right away with the case agent. He—it almost never would have been she in those days—would know the local territory thoroughly: its places, customs, and secrets. Once trust was gained, he could tell you many details that weren't included in the official reports in the case file. Most important of all, the case agent would know friends, colleagues, sources, and informants who wouldn't bare their souls to an outsider like me in a million years.

There would be no grand jury in Williamsport to call and recall witnesses, or to gather and sift evidence. I was counting heavily on this fellow for all the help I could get.

Unfortunately, Reese turned out to be less than useless. Sleepy-eyed, a bit slovenly in contrast to traditional Brooks Brothers Bureau standards, he was a study in sullen disinterest. He dutifully reviewed the file with me, but added almost nothing between the lines. There was no enthusiasm whatsoever. He provided me with all of the raw case notes and other documents I had requested, but there was no offer to help organize or explain them. I didn't expect every agent to be the second coming of Elliot Ness, but I found myself thinking, *Damn it man, I'm not asking for any favors here—this is your job.* After a couple of hours of this routine, I wasn't a happy camper, and he knew it. What the hell was going on here?

Slowly but surely, I got the picture. Reese explained that he knew that I'd been ordered by my bosses, for some reason, to push this silly case, and that he understood that it wasn't my fault. He had assumed this matter had died when both the local police and the U.S. Attorney declined prosecution. He mentioned that he had spoken with Denise Bishop, and that she was "a pain in the ass." In fact, she'd started in whining about how no one was doing anything about that "prank." Imagine that—get a lousy cross burned on your lawn, and you think you're the only one with a problem! Eventually, phrases like "dark meat" and "uppity" started coming out. Easy Howard, easy, I told myself. You're playing in his ballpark, and he's gone by the book on paper. No one will give a damn about your complaints about this guy's attitude. I had no trouble imagining my supervisors' response: "So he's an asshole—so what? He's not the first and he won't be the last. Who were you expecting, Nelson Mandela? Just get on with your job."

And of course my supervisor would be absolutely correct.

∽

At day's end, I finally met Denise Bishop. She had just arrived home after picking up her son after her workday at a Williamsport bank. My disappointment (make that disgust) with my FBI agent was 180 degrees opposite from delight with the demeanor of my star witness. She was attractive and impeccably dressed, but not distractingly so (such things are important to juries and judges). She was bright, articulate, and directly responsive to my questions. I don't believe I ever dealt with a key witness so poised, before or since. Her memory of the night in question matched the official reports in all material respects. For once, maybe I wouldn't need to beat my brains out preparing a scared, reluctant, victim, over and over, for the ordeal of trial.

But young Carl was another story. Slight, awkward, and shy, he seemed like he would rather be any place else in the world than discussing his Night From Hell with a complete stranger. His responses were short and mumbled, and he avoided my gaze. His mother shot me a couple of looks which I interpreted as "not now—don't make him go through that again." Clearly this was not yet the time to review the nightmare of the incident in question.

Our preliminary work finished, Denise Bishop insisted that I stay for dinner. One extra plate would be no trouble, she told me; it was the least she could do. Like me, she seemed tired and lonely. If the other restaurants within my meager government travel allowance were anything like the previous evening's dump, this wasn't a close call. The food and company were most pleasant, and when I started to stand up at 8:00 p.m. or so, I was once again asked to stay. It was tempting, but there were many good reasons not to. When on the road, we were considered to be representatives of the United States on a 24/7 basis. As lonesome and targeted as we usually were, we had been warned in no uncertain terms of the importance of keeping things strictly professional. The last thing this case needed was for the locals to see my car parked in the victim's driveway late at night. Wouldn't that look wonderful on cross-examination:

"Mrs. Bishop, did Mr. Feinstein instruct you as to your testimony today? No? Not even when he spent the night at your house?"

And off I went into the night, back to my roach motel on the outskirts of town.

Having devoured the federal and local case documents, and reviewed what little physical evidence still existed, I spent the remainder of that first trip, and several more, chasing leads and speaking with everyone I could find who might know anything, or anyone, relating to the case. I fast became a well-known presence in the community, going door to door and diner to diner in search of information. The telephones were buzzing, and everyone seemed to know who I was as soon as they answered the doorbell. I was hardly welcomed with open arms, but I suppose I represented some novelty in a town not exactly brimming with excitement. Most of the people I encountered were young and not particularly worldly. When one high school girl greeted me with "Oh, you must be that Jew from Washington," it sounded almost sweetly naïve.

Just about everyone who consented to talk with me, whether sympathetic or not, was stunned at this living example of wasted federal tax dollars: Washington sent you all the way up here for that stupid prank from last year?

The burnt cross was by now a local legend, and no one really denied that the incident took place. However, with the exception of one young girl who appeared to be struggling with her conscience, no one came forward with much in the way of useful information either. It was all pretty frustrating, and I finally reached the point when I realized that I wasn't going to extract any more blood from this particular turnip. It was time to get ready for trial.

∽

At a series of pre-trial meetings and conferences, I met the rest of the key players in this drama. Berofsky himself was a lanky, soft-spoken, rather nondescript individual. I attempted to draw him out to take his measure, but he wisely let his lawyer do most of the talking. He lacked the bravado of the Ku Klux Klan-style true believer. At the age of eight, he had barely escaped a house fire in which his father had perished, and he helped support himself and his widowed mother by working part-time jobs. He didn't resemble the personification of evil I was used to in cases like this. His attorney, Peter Campana, formerly the Lycoming County Public Defender, was sharp, confident, and honorable in all his dealings. His pretrial written submissions were first-rate—not always the case with the local lawyers we faced, who often lacked federal court experience—and he went out of his way to be cordial and hospitable to a fellow member of the bar far from home.

Once again, I got along better with opposing counsel than my so-called colleagues on the road, who seemed to resent my presence on their home turf. I never figured out the reason for this anomaly until years later, when I received a most logical explanation from a wise veteran prosecutor. She explained that a client under federal criminal investigation meant a nice piece of change for a local attorney, particularly in a low-income rural area. "It's a business out there, Howard. You might think of it as a noble profession, but out in the real world it's all about 'show me the money.'" Truer words were never spoken.

The real X-factor for me was Federal District Judge Malcolm Muir, a 67 year-old Nixon appointee, robust and strong of voice, with hardly any civil rights record in this heavily white neck of the woods. Because there were no juries in federal juvenile cases, he would not only make the usual trial rulings, but would issue the verdict. Our fate lay squarely in his hands. His reputation was that of a fair man, with no particular axe to grind. Thinking back to my days in the chambers of Judge Hand in Mobile, Alabama, where drawings of Robert E. Lee's Army of Northern Virginia adorned the walls, I reminded myself that I could do a lot worse.

Early in our initial conference, Judge Muir revealed that he was a longtime friend of Berofsky's family, and that Jon referred to him as "Uncle Malcolm." At this point, I tried hard to keep from fainting or crying. The judge explained, for my benefit, that in a small community like Williamsport, where almost everyone knew each other, these relationships were not uncommon. He would understand completely, however, if the Justice Department would prefer that he recuse himself from this case. I considered this briefly, but after a hasty consultation with an Assistant U.S. Attorney, I declined the offer. Any substitute judge would have to travel from Scranton or Harrisburg, delaying the trial and disrupting the new judge's schedule. And, I was informed, no judge's temperament was going to benefit from a trip to exotic Williamsport. I decided to take my chances with Judge Muir, hoping that he would bend over backward to resist any temptation toward personal bias.

Throughout the case, the courtroom was closed to the public and the media, standard practice for juvenile matters. Accordingly, press coverage was much more limited than I'm used to on the road. Furthermore, I was told, the town fathers were not anxious for the image of a burning cross in the All-American city to be transmitted over the wires, so soon after the annual economic boost provided by the Little League World Series. The trial proved to be refreshingly brief and to the point. With no jury to impress or inflame, there were far fewer objections, fiery harangues, and other typical courtroom theatrics than usual. Judge Muir was curt and sometimes impatient, but he was consistently neutral, never tipping his hand.

Denise Bishop was indeed a dream witness. She was unflinching under tough cross-examination, which gave her a second opportunity to point at Berofsky and identify him as her tormentor. And, bless her heart, she had saved the repair bills from her aluminum siding and her car, which came in as government exhibits. I also introduced the lease she broke when she moved out of her home not long following the cross-burning, along with the rental agreement for her new residence across the river. Our final exhibits were the canceled checks Mrs. Bishop had written to the security service she hired after the incident, for personal protection and to pick up Carl after school.

A succession of defense witnesses swore to Berofsky's upstanding, hard-working nature; his after-school employment to help support the family ever since the devastating fire; his clean record before and after the incident; and, of course, the required testament that he "didn't have a racist bone in his body." (At this point in my civil rights career, I would have dearly loved to have a dollar for every time I'd heard that phrase!). My cross-examination of these witnesses was minimal. I lacked the skill or experience to change their minds; I was hardly likely to succeed in getting them to admit that the defendant was, in fact, a hard-core racial bigot.

My most difficult strategic decision was whether or not to put Carl Bishop on the stand. He was my only eyewitness other than his mother, and despite his youth, he was a completely innocent, sympathetic figure. No attorney is comfortable with child witnesses, but I didn't have many alternatives. But Denise Bishop was adamant:

> "He's been through so much. He's lost his father. He's had three homes in the past year, and he's not exactly Mr. Popularity at school. He's had some emotional difficulties since the incident (who wouldn't, I thought), and he's finally started to work through them. He can't go through cross-examination—he's only

ten years old! You've got to do this without him."

I'd had similar conversations with reluctant—often terrified, with good reason—witnesses many times before, but never regarding anyone so young. I knew that even if I subpoenaed Carl and put him on, he'd probably be a nervous wreck. His mother would never forgive me, and I needed her to be 100% on board and a persuasive, sympathetic figure before the judge. Ultimately, I gave Carl a pass, surely violating the commandment in the prosecutor's bible to do "whatever it takes" to prepare a reluctant witness for trial. I prayed this would not doom our chances.

I felt fairly confident about the government's case, but without Carl Bishop our line-up was looking pretty thin. Fortunately, during my door-to-door amateur investigation, I stumbled upon one potentially promising witness, seventeen year-old Melanie Tovaris. While no more forthcoming than most of her contemporaries, who had little use for me, she seemed genuinely conflicted. She was practically the only person I spoke with who expressed sincere sympathy for the Bishops. I learned that she was an excellent student, and had an interest in seeing some of the world beyond Lycoming County, Pennsylvania one day. She was well acquainted with Berofsky, and by this time she knew all there was to know about the evening in question. But she was still a girl from the neighborhood, a close-knit community where you took care of your own, and you didn't tell tales out of school.

She was a convincing witness, nervously but clearly testifying that Berofsky had bragged to her about the cross-burning; that he had referred to the victim as "that colored bitch"; and that he had told Mrs. Bishop to "go back to Erie Avenue," a code-word for what passed for an

African-American area of Williamsport. She also recalled occasionally seeing Berofsky and his friends hurl rocks at Denise Bishop's cat and her house. Immediately following a grueling cross-examination, she left the witness stand shaken and walked out of the courtroom. I never saw her again, but I remember her as a true heroine. I'd be heading home to Washington shortly after the final gavel, on to my next case. But Melanie Tovaris would be returning to The Neighborhood, where I doubted things would ever be quite the same for her.

But my best witness was no one that I had summoned to the stand. It was Jon Berofsky himself, surely testifying over the objection of his wise defense attorney. This unworldly eighteen year-old had no place on a federal witness stand, but I certainly wasn't complaining. Through absolutely no brilliance of my own, the government struck gold. Sometimes, it's better to be lucky than good.

CROSS-EXAMINATION OF DEFENDANT JON BEROFSKY

Q. You stated in your direct testimony that this incident was just a prank. You've pulled pranks before, haven't you?

A. I guess so.

Q. Did you burn a cross in any of those?

A. I guess not.

Q. What did you do for those other pranks?

A. I don't remember.

Q. Well, did you throw eggs at someone's house, or paper a house with toilet paper, or maybe spray someone with shaving cream—things like that?

A. Yeah, I guess so.

Q. But you didn't do any of those things to Mrs. Bishop, did you?

DEFENSE COUNSEL: Objection, Your Honor. Mr. Feinstein is repeating the same question over and over, and he's badgering the witness.

JUDGE MUIR: There's no jury here, so I'll allow this line of questioning, but Mr. Feinstein, let's move it along.

Q. So, please tell us why this was the only occasion that you chose to burn a cross?

A. I don't know.

Q. Had you ever seen a burning cross before?

A. I guess so.

Q. Where did you see it?

A. Maybe on TV.

Q. And what television show would this have been?

DEFENSE COUNSEL: Your Honor, really --

JUDGE MUIR: Mr. Feinstein, you are starting to try my patience.

Q. I'm almost finished, Your Honor. Mr. Berofsky, please answer the question.

A. I think maybe it was a documentary about some group.

Q. And what group was that?

A. I don't remember. Maybe something like the Ku Klux Klan.

Q. I see. The Ku Klux Klan, which hates and intimidates

black people and other minorities, right?

A. Yeah, I guess so.

Q. So, how do you think Mrs. Bishop felt when she looked out her window and saw the burning cross that you'd planted on her lawn?

A. I don't know.

Q. Come on now, Mr. Berofsky, what do you think that burning cross meant to Mrs. Bishop?

A. Well, I guess it meant terroristic threats against American Negroes.

PROSECUTION: No further questions, Your Honor.

At this point, I stole a quick glance at defense attorney Campana. He looked as though he'd just received a call from his doctor informing him of a terminal illness. For me, it was more than just the gratification of winning the age-old courtroom battle of egos. I now had in the record, in the defendant's own words, specific evidence of the racial intimidation required by the fair housing law. This should prove enormously helpful in swaying not only Judge Muir, but for any subsequent appellate review. At the close of trial, Judge Muir took the case under advisement, telling us he would issue a ruling in a week or so. After the defendant's testimony, I was feeling fairly confident, but I had learned the hard way that in the civil rights arena, you never counted your chickens before they hatched.

It was indeed a nerve-racking week of waiting, but Judge Muir did the right thing. If anything, his written decision was even stronger than the trial brief I had submitted. I was sure that Peter Campana would never forget seeing his client's memorable phrase, "Terroristic threats against American Negroes," highlighted in the court's opinion. I certainly could not have said it better myself. All that remained was sentencing, an anticlimactic but necessary last step.

Our sentencing trips tended to be relatively low-pressure affairs, and sometimes occasions for a celebration by the trial team. In the federal system, the judges were responsible for sentencing, and they generally had made up their minds prior to the hearings. This time, the sentencing conference, in which each side expressed their recommendations, took place on a late Friday afternoon, with the hearing set for early Monday morning. It was going to be another fun-filled weekend in dreary Williamsport, my very own Paris-On-The-Susquehanna. Any inclination to go exploring was quickly put to rest, as I received several typically obnoxious, anonymous threats. But, as Dan Rinzel, Chief of the Criminal Section, reminded me:

"If no one's threatening you or complaining to Washington about you, then you probably aren't doing an aggressive enough job."

Good point, boss.

In federal juvenile matters, when the victim had suffered no physical injury and the defendant had no prior criminal record, a probationary sentence was all but guaranteed. Predictably, Jon Berofsky received one year of federal probation, and, at our request, was ordered to pay restitution to Mrs. Bishop to cover her moving expenses and forfeited rental deposit. I wasn't surprised, but I wasn't thrilled either. I find that I have very little of that admirable quality known as "mercy" when it comes to these cases. My friend and fellow keyboard man, Daryl Davis, wrote an amazing book, *Klan-Destine Relationships: A Black Man's Odyssey In The Ku Klux Klan*, detailing his efforts to get to know these folks as individuals, at considerable personal risk, in order to increase understanding on all sides. I sincerely admire this sense of compassionate empathy, but I just cannot bring myself to partake of it. I just can't do it—I want to see them all burn in Hell. Call me a vindictive SOB; I plead guilty.

Denise Bishop, demonstrating far more compassion than I, was satisfied, and that was probably the most important thing. She had no interest in seeing a kid go to prison. She insisted that all she ever wanted was for this matter to be taken seriously—*for attention to be paid.*

Despite the just ending to this case, few of its cast of characters lived happily ever after. Jon Berofsky tried a variety of different vocations, eventually leaving town. He owns a small business, several states away. He has stayed below the radar and off the police blotter. Did he learn his lesson? Who knows? He apparently learned to stay out of trouble—whether or not he ever developed any sensitivity to the rights of minorities is anyone's guess.

Denise Bishop, to no one's surprise, did not settle down in Williamsport for the long run. She kept moving from town to town, state to state, job to job, marriage to marriage, never quite finding security or inner peace in these United States.

Who knows what demons that burning cross in the night spawned in Carl Bishop? He stayed on the move with his mother, never knowing the comfort of a permanent neighborhood or a loyal group of friends. He never really discovered his niche, and began running with a rough crowd. Several stops later on his journey, in New York City, he was a defendant in a brutal, highly-publicized murder case. Against all odds, he was acquitted. It was neither his first, nor his last, brush with the law.

Craig Reese, my reluctant, narrow-minded case agent, was not long for the FBI career fast-track. He was disciplined for using his official vehicle for religious proselytizing. In the straight-arrow, unforgiving culture of the Bureau, one did not rebound easily from such blemishes on your permanent record. If Reese thought Williamsport was cold, I wonder how he enjoyed winter at the Fargo and Fairbanks bureau field offices.

Linda Davis, whose tenacity rescued this case from the ash-heap of Closed Files, was eventually promoted to Chief of the Criminal Section. She is now a Senior Associate Judge of the Superior Court of the District of Columbia.

Not much has changed in South Williamsport. The Little League World Series still comes to town every August, pouring money into the local economy and spreading the town's All-American image across television screens nationwide. Other than that, there's still precious little to keep bored teenagers productively occupied in the evenings. These days, there's a fire station behind the little house on Main Street, way too late to douse that fiery cross. And unlike, say, Rosa Parks, Denise Bishop's courage did not exactly spark a revolution. Census figures indicate that there are zero African-Americans in town.

And Judge Muir? He continued to hear cases until the age of 96, when he died peacefully, at work in his chambers. They don't make Republicans like him any more.

Howard L. Feinstein

Fire on the Bayou

The Long and Winding Road

For most of my time on official travel, I found myself in the Deep South: the Gulf Coast, the lowlands, the swamps, the bottoms—a subtropical steam bath. This meant unrelenting heat and humidity. Non-stop, 24-hour, strength-sapping, dehydrating, glasses-fogging, clothes-soaking, temper-shortening, road-melting, hot-to-the-touch, will-wilting, matter-over-mind heat. We wore the requisite suits and ties, our female colleagues "dressed for success," carrying boxes of documents and briefcases, driving the cheapest possible rental cars (sometimes called "U-Drive-Its" down South) with scalding interiors and problematical air-conditioning; waiting in boiling airport lost-luggage rooms, on claustrophobic small airplanes grounded on runways; marking time in rural diners with ancient ceiling fans; and patronizing filthy, steaming laundromats. At night, we experienced the delights of swarms of angry insects; vapors rising off the bayous and rivers; and cheap, decaying motel rooms with struggling cooling systems. Add to this the pervasive smells of wood pulp, turpentine, creosote, sulfur, and other noxious substances in Southern mill and industrial towns, as yet untouched by environmental regulation. Forever baking in the oven, we continually fought to hold back a rising tide of lethargy.

On the road we were predominantly-white knights, battling the forces of evil. It was crucial to keep this romantic sense of glorious mission in the forefront of our consciousness, as it carried us through an undeniably shabby daily existence. We were the Army of the Second Reconstruction, similarly foreign and just as convinced of our righteousness. Back home, we were part of the vast legion of government employees in the Capital, faceless civil servants blending in with the rest of the indigenous population. But "on travel," we were the center of attention, sought after by the media, seen on the local television news, and quoted in the newspapers—heady wine for young, ambitious lawyers. We were, too, mercifully out from under the Justice Department bureaucracy and its none-too-gentle supervisory hierarchy. There were no cell phones, no computers, no smart phones or Blackberries, no e-mail, no faxes—even phone booths were few and far between in rural areas. We called in to Washington when we had the opportunity, but many critical decisions were made on the fly, the product of our own inexperienced judgment. It was on-the-job-training, not to be found in any instructional manual; it was sink-orswim, preferably the latter. We were an expeditionary force, living off the land in the pre-digital age—most definitely behind the lines.

Not long after arrival in the usual down-home locale, the transformation from a heretofore written case-file to reality was a sudden shock to the system. The star witness who came across as articulate in written reports was sullen and reeking of alcohol at 10:00 a.m. in person. The victim of racial harassment or police brutality, a sympathetic hero in the case file, was mistrustful of our intentions and thoroughly sick of the whole situation. In criminal matters, the FBI agents we were critically dependent upon could be anywhere from lazy, or outright hostile, to a godsend of local knowledge and resourcefulness. The local United States Attorney's Office, generally our only realistic prospect for logistical support and creature comforts, spanned the full range from friend to foe. I spent a good deal of time in the Southern District of Alabama, where my involvement in a long-standing, highly visible school desegregation case was deemed so invasive by my fellow federal prosecutors that I was made to draft documents and conduct research while sitting in a chair in a hallway. The mighty emissary of the all-powerful Justice Department looked like a grade-school child being punished for classroom misbehavior. For once holding my tongue, I resisted the temptation to remind the U.S. Attorney that both of our paychecks were signed by Uncle Sam.

There was no way around it: our travel accommodations were pitiful. Official limits on travel expenses (these were written in stone—any appeal would have been deemed laughable) were such that, even when our destinations offered a choice of motels, we still had to stay in dumps. Most of us were young attorneys, starting families, at the lower end of the modest government salary scale (no special pay-scale for lawyers existed then or now). Paying a portion of the expenses ourselves was not a feasible option. The notion of overtime or comptime pay might as well have been science fiction. Our expense reimbursement requests were reviewed with an extremely fine-toothed comb. I recall having my morning coffee disallowed ("You could have had a free cup of coffee on the flight home"). This was always a morale booster on the heels of a two-week stay in Lackluster, Arkansas.

The official per diem allowance almost always meant a choice between (a) three decent meals, or (b) a vaguely clean and/or safe place to stay. The long hours and constant travel left us fairly depleted of much-needed energy, so we generally opted for the food. We shared intelligence on "all you can eat" establishments, and, in more urban areas, bars with free happy-hour hors d'oeuvres. (Our welcome wore out quickly at those places. Thinking back on it, we should have worn disguises on return visits.) An up-to-date list of motels relatively free from disease and violence was also maintained in the office. This institutional knowledge served as a valuable lifeline. Without it, how could I have known to avoid Days Inn during its unfortunate period of electrocutions from faulty pool lighting? We grew quite used to dim, flickering lighting; phantom air-conditioning; thriving colonies (Mobile, Alabama, my home away from home for many months, featured the "Roachway Inn"); filthy, Depression-era beds and furniture; noisome sexual athletes and angry combatants in neighboring rooms; nonstop, pounding bass lines from ground-floor discos; and always, the least possible assistance or service, given that we were about as welcome as IRS auditors.

Of course, any call back to Mother Justice to complain of local inconveniences was viewed as a pathetic sign of weakness. This went well beyond the standard legal credo, unchallenged in the arena of litigation, of "Never show weakness; never let them see you sweat." We were expected to grin and bear it at all times, certainly when getting hammered by hostile federal judges, as I often was. Back home, we were reminded regularly of the tradition we were upholding, dating back to the older, more dangerous days. Back then, Civil Rights Division attorneys drove the back roads (never at night) with tire irons on the passenger seat, calling in to headquarters every hour to let Washington know they were alive and well. I can't say that I never complained, but I received, and deserved, no sympathy. It was what I signed on for, period.

My efforts to "blend in" on the road, or at least to not appear too exotic, usually proved fruitless. My Criminal Section chief jokingly suggested that I drop "Feinstein" and go by my given names, Howard Lee ("Sure Dan, I'm sure I'll pass as a local Southern Baptist farmer."). My hair was long and unruly in those days, true to my anti-authoritarian, California roots. But on official travel, I sported an investigative, grand jury, or trial haircut, depending upon the nature of the trip. Eventually I realized that, above all, I had to slow down. My Yankee, lawyer-like propensity to cut to the chase and zero in on the facts of the case was not working. Rapport, relaxation, pace—all had to be re-tooled, in order to gain trust. On the other hand, I was indisputably rushed. Living in shabby motels with mediocre, intermittent meals, far from my wife and young children, it was very difficult to mask my impatience with the road and my desire to Get The Hell Out Of Here. Many was the trip where the government's interests would have been better served had I stayed an extra day or two.

Never exactly a people person, I gradually learned to relax and feel more comfortable with personal conversation on the road. However, I also came to realize the pitfalls of revealing too much. Airborne discussions with fellow passengers regarding the nature of my travels yielded too many responses along the lines of Martin Luther King deserving his fate, along with his obvious Communist beliefs. The discovery that I was a Justice Department attorney redressing a local civil rights grievance was often characterized as not only misguided, but a classic example of tax dollars put to hideous waste. I found that unless absolutely necessary for official purposes, it was best not to mention my name. Discussions of general ethnic characteristics; World Jewry: Its Leaders and Objectives; Jews I Have Known; and similar conversational topics grew a tad tiresome. Perhaps my Criminal Section chief was correct after all—few surnames were as palatable as Lee below the Mason-Dixon Line.

We worked very hard on the road, much more so than in Washington. With the spectacular exception of New Orleans—paradise for a musician like me—there was very little to distract us from the task at hand. Busy all day with court, grand jury, depositions, negotiations, interviews, and endless driving down questionable roads, we prepared, strategized, and drafted documents long into the night. This was just as well, as we were specifically advised to keep a low profile in many locations, due to our unpopularity, both North and South. Driving GSA cars (decrepit Fords and Chevrolets from the federal motor pool, which were just short of Last Rites), dressing like carpetbaggers, and speaking with strange accents, our presence did not long remain secret. Not every greeting was as overtly threatening as that in Willacoochee, but the occasional racist or anti-Semitic phone message was not that rare. People had a way of discovering where we were staying and when we were arriving, and I soon learned not to use my real name in motel registers.

Everyone understood that no indiscretion of any kind would be tolerated while on travel. No matter how significant or routine the particular matter at hand, we were considered official government representatives at all times. Everyone knew the legendary tales of government attorneys found in hotel rooms with drugs of various kinds, prostitutes, or locally acquired paramours; the Justice Department lawyer who drank a beer during a deposition, or exposed him or herself during Mardi Gras in New Orleans, etc. Each of these stories, true, exaggerated, or mythical, culminated in swift separation from public service and irrevocable professional disgrace. I was no angel, but it just wasn't worth the risk.

"Weren't you afraid?" has always been the most frequently-asked question concerning those days. I was lucky. Other than periodic covert threats or public demonstrations of ill will, I never suffered any physical harm during my civil rights travels. This changed later in my career, when I was mugged and manhandled outside a downtown Los Angeles hotel. I suppose I was so used to the strict limits on travel expenses from my Justice Department days that I never did learn to upgrade. Young and full of ourselves, we surely wore these threats as potential, if unrealized, as badges of honor.

Of course, not everyone touched by the civil rights movement would emerge unscathed. Sometimes the piper was paid immediately, like the victims in my Ku Klux Klan and murder cases. But sometimes payment came due later. The year after I left the Civil Rights Division, I participated in a federal appellate argument in Atlanta. One of the judges on my hearing panel, Robert Vance of Alabama, had been one of the true judicial heroes of the civil rights movement earlier in his career, courageously upholding the Constitution and federal laws in the face of considerable unpopularity. Not long after my hearing, he was killed, and his wife severely injured, by a letter bomb mailed by a vengeful, unrepentant from the bad old days, Le Roy Moody, Jr. We may move on from the civil rights arena, but it always remains a part of us, for better or for worse.

∽

Hartford, Connecticut was my all-time least favorite travel destination. My northernmost stop, it was forever freezing, windy, dark and dreary, and something always went wrong. Things got rolling with the treacherous, icy drive from the distant airport at night in heavy traffic. Ancient, drafty hotels seemed to consistently misplace my reservation. There was absolutely nothing to do on the rare occasions when I had the time: the roof of the Civic Center, venue for indoor local musical and athletic events, had collapsed from heavy snowfall.

Fire on the Bayou

One night I was wakened in the pre-dawn hours by vigorous pounding on the door of my low-rent airport motel room ("Prostitutes always welcome; inquire about our hourly rates"). I was confused, scared, and momentarily not sure where I was and what the hell I was doing there. It was the local police, inquiring as to my whereabouts earlier in the evening, when the night clerk unfortunately became a fatal victim of an armed robbery at the front desk. I came to my senses quickly enough to display my Justice Department credentials, sarcastically noting that, as a federal prosecutor, I was probably not high on their list of prime suspects. Predictably, like law enforcement officers everywhere, they were not amused.

My traveling companion, a young paralegal in the next room who was new to the glamour of government travel, needed a fair amount of calming down. Unfortunately, my well-intentioned assurances of safety dissipated soon afterward, when we exited through the lobby and viewed the yellow crime-scene tape surrounding a chalk outline of the body. This incident was the source of considerable amusement later that day at the United States Attorney's office, where federal prosecutors immediately recognized our accommodations as a notorious drug-buy location. No one could believe that we had actually stayed there. Apparently, they had yet to experience the joys of traveling on Uncle Sam's nickel.

On the positive side, I did meet some fine people in the Hartford area, who extended me some much-needed good will. As isolated and exhausted as we were, it was always a pleasure to experience hospitality on the road. In Hartford, I got to know my opposing attorney, Dominic Squatrito—now a federal district judge—quite well. He was unfailingly courteous and personable, despite our being on opposite sides of some highly contentious and public litigation. The ability to separate the personal from the official was a critical attribute for any attorney. This often proved difficult for me, with my ready demonization of all associated with The Other Side in civil rights matters. I remember to this day Judge Squatrito's description of his religious and ethnic identification. He dearly loved being an Italian-American Roman Catholic, faithfully attending mass, christenings, communions, festivals, saint's day celebrations, and other rituals. However, he added, "All that doesn't make me any better than anyone else." Did I hear this correctly? What a refreshing outlook.

Fort Pierce was a picturesque Florida beach town and baseball spring training site—a welcome break from the Washington winter. My case was a never-ending, bitterly litigated school desegregation battle that had divided the community into hostile camps. Like many of these cases, it was eventually settled after lengthy negotiations. But for a long stretch, things were nasty indeed. One afternoon, as I left the federal courthouse following a hearing on a proposed elementary school integration plan, passions overflowed. A sign-carrying crowd of angry parents, enraged by the prospect of the b-word (bussing), yelled, booed, and hissed expletives at me. This was followed by the hurling of paper cups, wadded-up tissues, and other mercifully soft objects in my direction. Guided by a local attorney, I made haste for my car and drove away, shaken but not stirred to any response. After all, any report to my superiors in Washington would have been seen as hopeless whining, eliciting the standard response of, "So what? You're down there to enforce the law, not to win popularity contests." And they would have been right.

∼

Wheeling, West Virginia: Appalachia. A police brutality prosecution (three separate incidents involving the same officer), with, for a change, no racial aspect—everyone involved was poor and white. One of my first criminal cases, I was serving as "second chair" with a veteran female prosecutor. We conducted repeated interviews with victims, witnesses, and other down-and-out residents in dilapidated, weather-beaten cottages on an island in the Ohio River. All was gray: the sky, the houses, the people—a truly bleak setting. Our key victim, Danny Hayes, was particularly unhelpful, ignoring our questions, cracking jokes, and plowing his way through a six-pack late in the muggy morning. Eventually, realizing that it would be only fair to offer his personal contribution to this strategy session, Danny turned to the pair of emissaries from the nation's capital and inquired, "Are you two staying in the same room? Are you fucking her?"

Undaunted, we continued preparations on the day before trial, when we reviewed basic courtroom procedures. When we explained the ritual of standing when the judge entered the courtroom, Danny, an independent soul unbound by tradition, exploded: "What? Man, that's fucking bullshit! Everybody knows me, I'm Danny Hayes from The Island. I don't have to kiss any judge's ass!" We dutifully informed our witness that the federal judge presiding over the case was, in fact unlikely to have traveled in Danny's circles, and that standing was merely a formality, rather than a symbol of inferiority. Unfortunately, this explanation proved wholly unconvincing, and we moved onto a variation on the standard speech we had all given from time to time in these circumstances: "Two government attorneys have traveled all the way here from Washington, D.C. to protect your rights. Is it really too much to ask that you stand up for five seconds at the beginning of each day?"

Yes, it was. Not guilty on all counts. After the verdict, the judge invited us into his chambers to commiserate, stating that the police officer was clearly guilty, and that we had done our best with what evidence we had. It was a most charitable thing to say, and it certainly wasn't what we expected to hear back at the office. Several years later, I had the opposite experience, when a Louisiana jury convicted a deputy sheriff of racially motivated police brutality, overriding the persistent views of the trial judge to the contrary. That one felt a whole lot better.

Taking a break to work off the tension during a long trip involving the desegregation of several East Texas school districts, I ran a few miles in a field adjacent to my Tyler, Texas motel. As I walked back through the lobby on my way to my room for a quick shower, the desk clerk, who had seen me head out to run a half-hour ago, casually mentioned that particular field had been known to be infested with snakes. I was always the naïve outsider.

Stuck inside of Mobile with the Memphis blues again. I probably spent more time here than at any other destination. The Mobile County school case seemed interminable. Indeed, it was one of the oldest desegregation cases in the country, originally brought by Thurgood Marshall. Now there was a standard I would never live up to. I also had a few smaller matters near Mobile, and I believed I could still easily drive around without a map. Decades later, I received more hospitality, from several quarters, here more than anywhere else. A periodic dinner guest at the homes of private attorneys on all sides of the school case, as well as civil rights activists, I often dined and drank in good company, a rarity on the road. Mobile was the proud home to the nation's first Mardi Gras, predating New Orleans, and it had some decent places to eat, but there wasn't much else going on. I watched so many Atlanta Braves games on television that I memorized their entire roster, including uniform numbers and vital statistics.

The enforcement stage of the school desegregation case dragged on for several years, as we negotiated the details of a workable, legally satisfactory plan. These discussions took place at Barton Academy, which had previously served as a Confederate hospital during the Civil War. This was a nice match for the portraits of Confederate generals in the chambers of the judge presiding. Finally, we reached preliminary agreement on a desegregation plan, and I testified, before the school board, whose president, a fellow member of the bar, was my chief adversary. Some years later, he would serve four years in federal prison for his part in a kickback scheme for school construction contracts. No doubt some of these contracts were for new buildings and renovations required by our plan. Thank God I didn't have to testify in that case.

Having disregarded the speed limit once again one blazing Friday afternoon, in a desperate attempt to make the day's last possible flight home, I rudely ran to the front of the airport check-in line and flashed my official credentials. The shaken clerk let me through, asking whether I was armed. My Justice Department badge had bailed me out of more than one traffic ticket—occasionally I wondered whether I was being granted professional courtesy by a police officer I might end up prosecuting some day. Rank has its privileges. I took my small pleasures where I could find them on the road.

Being somewhat anti-social by nature, and a known figure in the city of Mobile due to the notoriety of the desegregation case, I sometimes retreated to the "Redneck Riviera" on the Gulf, when I had to stay over on weekends. The casual, beachfront atmosphere offered a welcome tonic. At lunch one lazy Sunday in a pleasant watering hole, I encountered none other than "The Snake" himself, Kenny Stabler, pro football luminary back in my native San Francisco Bay Area. Alabama was, and remains, unsurpassed as football country. Every attorney and public official I met wore either an Alabama or Auburn class ring, and Kenny remained a deity in his home state, where he starred for Alabama under the state's most revered figure, Coach Bear Bryant. Seeing The Snake hold court at his table before a parade of worshipful admirers, I wistfully put things in perspective. Lawsuits, even those lasting several decades and affecting every citizen in the largest school district in the state, may come and go, but Kenny and his brethren would never have to pay for a drink in these parts.

Fire on the Bayou

Greater Houston, the nation's fastest-growing metropolitan area, was the site of many of my most interesting cases, but it was also the most exhausting place imaginable to navigate. Sprawling (to put it mildly), confusing, and lacking in zoning regulations, it had almost no public transportation. It was Los Angeles with humidity. Driving and parking were a constant challenge, and it was expensive enough that we always came out on the short end on travel expenses. We came to know the downtown bars with free happy-hour snacks, the cut-rate Mexican diners, and the all-you-can-eat ptomaine palaces just off the interstates. Still, we could afford only motels for which terms like "questionable" or "in transition" were nice ways of putting it.

This was the site of my first school desegregation case, in a huge district with a vocal black community. We met with community leaders in an African American funeral home, planning strategy and listening to local concerns while mourners wailed audibly in adjoining rooms. We were constrained by prevailing federal statutes and court decisions, and our roles did not always mesh perfectly with the aims of the community, which, after all, would have to live with the results. Gaining trust was challenging: we were told that the school superintendent had warned community leaders that, when push came to shove, *those white attorneys from Washington are not going to side with you black folks.* We were also informed that the hotel we stayed at (those generous government travel allowances again) had previously been the site of a slave market. What delightfully educational local history.

We ultimately prevailed after a grueling trial, but I learned—the hard way, as usual—that no matter how much preparation time I put in, your own witnesses will surely surprise you. One woman, describing her shock at realizing how poorly the all-black public schools had prepared her for college, testified that upon graduating with a high class standing from high school, she had thought she was "shit in high cotton." This phrase, not unfamiliar in Texas, evoked only mild laughter in the courtroom, but I turned bright red. In the official transcript, it came out as "shitting in high cotton." Of such elegant courtroom colloquy is constitutional law made. When the trial finally ended, and the judge made it clear that he would issue a ruling requiring desegregation, the lead attorney for the school district told us that, while he regretted the end of the old system, "at least now maybe some of these colored kids can get football scholarships to better colleges."

There you had it, in a nutshell. Apparently it was no longer possible to stop a bunch of carpetbaggers from forcing Texas to abide by the Constitution, but every cloud had its silver lining: maybe Texas A&M could make it to the Cotton Bowl more often now.

Sporting garish lipstick and dollar-store costume jewelry, well-worn high-heels clicking on the chipped walkway leading to our motel, a couple of world-weary ladies of the evening gave us a friendly Texas welcome:

"Hi there. Are you boys in from out of town?"

"No, we live down the street, but we enjoy wearing suits and ties and hauling luggage, briefcases, and thirty-pound boxes of documents around in this 98-degree heat."

∽

Cerro Maravilla, Puerto Rico, was the most exotic, intense, and explosive case in the island's volatile history. I felt like I was truly in the belly of the beast. I never worked so hard, but I never felt completely on top of things either. I was always playing catch-up, a stranger in a strange land. I was working at my peak, but for the first time in my career, I began to wonder whether my peak was good enough. Some years back, two young *independentistas*, on their way to blow up telephone relay towers in the mountainous jungle at the center of the island, were apprehended and executed by the Police of Puerto Rico. The official cover story—that the youths were surprised by the police, who shot them while returning fire—stood up for a long time, but ultimately began to break down from a steady trickle of leaks and tips.

Inconveniently for us, the sole neutral eye-witness was Negrito ("Blackie"), a guard dog at the telephone tower compound. While the Senate of Puerto Rico held daily, Watergate-style televised hearings that transfixed the entire island, we made repeated back-and-forth trips in an attempt to determine the truth, primarily using the federal grand jury process.

Cerro Maravilla (loosely translated as "marvelous mountain") was the most sensational legal matter in the history of an island already obsessed with the "status question": whether Puerto Rico should remain an American commonwealth, become the 51st state, or be an independent nation. This issue dominates the life of the island to this day. Everyone had a view on this case, and there was no reluctance to share those views with us. A high-ranking official in the San Juan F.B.I. office, an Anglo, told me in an unguarded moment that our efforts to uncover the truth could set back the cause of statehood by fifty years. The law enforcement officers assigned to protect us were colleagues, sometimes friends, of our targets. Everyone was armed and on guard. At the arraignment, I stood next to an officer who had blown one victim's brains out at close range in what proved to be an execution by firing-squad. His chilling glare, directed at my fellow prosecutor and me, was echoed by his numerous colleagues in the courtroom. Remember, Howard: Never let them see you sweat.

The pace was exhausting. All testimony took twice as long as usual, to allow for both Spanish and English translation. My own pathetic Spanish, adequate for asking directions or ordering meals, but not for interviewing reluctant witnesses, was a definite handicap. Threats, rumors, dead-end leads, and questionable strategy suggestions flew nonstop. Our superiors came down from Washington periodically to make sure we weren't making a difficult situation any worse. I couldn't blame them. Early one morning at the F.B.I. office in San Juan, following a long night of preparation, I had to be shaken awake by my tireless senior colleague Steve Clark, a Marine Corps combat veteran and true stand-up guy. A challenge like this was standard procedure for Steve, who had lived out of his hip pocket as a platoon leader in Vietnam. As for me: it wasn't my finest hour.

Through the use of tearful, often courageous secret grand jury testimony, gut-wrenching polygraph examinations, and our good fortune, we indicted ten police officers, all of whom were eventually convicted and incarcerated. It was a major victory for the forces of truth and justice, but it took its toll on me. I don't think I was ever the same after this marathon pressure cooker of a case. The constant travel and unrelenting pressure contributed significantly to my eventual transition to the less compelling regions of the civil rights battlefront.

For the vast majority of my cases, particularly early in my career, when the South still carried the vestiges of an underdeveloped country in our midst, most everyone we dealt with, whether white, black, or brown, was not too well off. In police brutality matters, as our supervisors accurately warned us, victims and witnesses were not often pillars of the community. Cross-burnings and Ku Klux Klan activity seldom occurred on the right side of the tracks. In school desegregation cases, many families with financial means had fled the public school system for the refuge of private "seg academies." But Marion County, in central Florida, was an eye-opener. I had never, professionally or personally, seen such staggering contrasts in socioeconomic status at this close range.

This was horse country. There were miles of gleaming white fences and winding trails, with thoroughbreds, some bound for Triple Crown competition, lazing and prancing under the white-hot skies. Scattered amidst the lakes were Florida's famed springs, with tourists lined up to descend beneath the surface to view spectacular marine life. Disney World and the attractions of Orlando beckoned nearby. I was no longer in the Old South I had grown used to; this was the Sunbelt, and it was booming.

But the black neighborhoods of Ocala, the county seat, were home to the most miserable poverty I had ever seen—and by this time I had seen plenty. Downcast families sat listlessly in front of their houses on sweltering summer evenings, along unimproved roads with no working streetlights. The last trash pick-up appeared to have been a month ago. The paint was almost completely gone from the elementary schools, whose playgrounds were filled with debris. There was no air conditioning. The Voting Rights Act of 1965, which we were supposed to be enforcing, had clearly not yet had any effect. The residents seemed utterly powerless in their own community. I knew that I was supposed to put my personal feelings aside and just do my job, but I felt like a suburban Afrikaner slumming in Soweto Township in the heyday of apartheid.

The attorney for the school district, a courtly gentleman, expressed his sympathy for my plight as a fellow Caucasian. Lawyer to lawyer, he understood perfectly that I had a client to represent, no matter how misguided. The Supreme Court had indeed ruled that all-white schools could not stand forever, and I had a job to do, my personal feelings notwithstanding. He noted that his daughter attended a high school that had recently been partially desegregated. She had come to learn, he explained, the true pathological nature of the Negro race firsthand. Apparently, I came to understand, the rule of law might inevitably triumph, but I didn't figure to have much impact on the fundamental human equation.

My comrade and I are were in the home stretch of the usual trial-eve push, before a morning hearing on integration of the Marion County elementary schools, so fiercely resisted by the local powers that be. Irresponsibly, we took time out to watch the Major League Baseball All-Star Game. This inevitably transformed the standard short evening of sleep into a classic all-nighter. At about 3:00 a.m., desperate for any help in the battle against sleepiness, we went down to the lobby and woke the night clerk, seeking replacement light bulbs, perhaps some even brighter than 40 watts. This poor gent, dazed and confused, had seen it all in his time. Still, he informed us, "That's one request I've never heard before."

∼

I learned some lessons the hard way in Corpus Christi. I appeared before Federal District Judge Hayden Head on several criminal matters. He also took over the lengthy Corpus Christi school desegregation suit, the first in the nation to hold that Hispanic students were entitled to a desegregated public education. Judge Head, while undeniably intelligent and hard-working, was absolute death on attorneys venturing into his courtroom, especially carpetbaggers such as yours truly. He had gone so far as to place signs at strategic points in his courtroom, warning lawyers of the consequences of various forms of inappropriate conduct. I always made sure to arrive early for his cases, for fear of being held in contempt and finding myself in the friendly confines of the courthouse lock-up.

Flying in the night before one hearing (I had already learned the danger of arriving on the day of a court appearance; federal judges were not interested in hearing about flight delays), I felt relatively confident, except for the seemingly minor inconvenience of my missing luggage. The following morning, my increasingly frantic calls to the airline were still to no avail. Two hours before the hearing time, I was sweating like a dog, recalling the guillotine scenes from A Tale of Two Cities. The prospect of appearing before Judge Head in jeans and sport-shirt brought visions of alternative professions to mind. When my suitcase finally arrived at the motel with little time to spare, I promised myself to go with the carry-on option for the remainder of my time on this Earth.

During negotiations on the desegregation case, I casually mentioned the name of a local architect who was helping us design a plan to reconfigure school zones and building usage in order to maximize integration. I thought nothing of it, but afterward, the attorney for the private plaintiffs let me know in no uncertain terms that I needed to watch what I said. Yet again, I was reminded that to a temporary visitor like me, these might be matters of numbers, policies, and maps. But on the ground, in Corpus Christi and elsewhere, they involved real people who walked tightropes that I could truly not fathom. In most of these communities, everyone knew everybody else, and there were no secrets when it came to the question of which side one was on. A job, a mortgage, or a life could be lost by siding with the Feds.

Of course, I should have known this by now. So many times, I had to interview potential witnesses after dark, beyond the town limits. Sometimes, these witnesses cried, trembled, or broke down. It was critical for me to understand and deal with their individual pressure points. While I might ultimately have the power of subpoena, cases were seldom won with reluctant, frightened witnesses. And above all, I could never overpromise. Television dramas to the contrary, not everyone could enter the federal witness protection program. I always carried that return ticket-to-ride in my pocket. For everyone else, consequences could be dire and permanent.

Very late one night in Corpus Christi, gale-force winds howled off the Gulf through the overmatched windows of our motel. Two Texas-based federal prosecutors and I were trying to wind up a strategy session on the eve of the trial of a small-town lawman accused of fatally beating a prisoner in his custody. At this point, we were walking zombies, floating between night and day, arguing over everything under the sun, all of us short of sleep, temper, and judgment.

Suddenly, the headboard of the bed in the room next door started steadily slamming into the wall. As this continued for several more minutes, we looked up from our massive mounds of paper, looked quizzically at each other, and simultaneously erupted into uncontrolled laughter, documents, pens, and file folders scattering to the floor. We were on the job indeed, on the road again. As our bosses never tired of telling us, "It's a privilege to be able to work on these cases." Well, that might be true, but that wasn't what cheap motels were meant for.

Fire on the Bayou

House-Hunting While Black

In addition to prosecuting Ku Klux Klan campaigns and other cases of interference with fair housing, the Criminal Section handled a large number of investigations into official misconduct. These generally involved police brutality, often with a racial aspect. These were very difficult cases in which to gain convictions, because juries just did not—and still don't—like to convict police officers. Even jurors not particularly inclined toward civil rights tend not to identify or sympathize with hooded terrorists or cross-burners. Policemen, on the other hand, were viewed as public servants performing dangerous, not particularly well-paid jobs. Law enforcement officers were experienced, relatively well-spoken witnesses, who were used to hostile cross-examination; they know how to act and look in a courtroom. Unlike many Klansmen and their fellow travelers, they had no criminal records, and could usually testify to years of service to their communities, on and off the job.

Perhaps most important of all, the victims in police misconduct cases were seldom, as our supervisors constantly reminded us, "pillars of the community." Anyone suffering the horror of having a cross burned on his or her property would generally be viewed as an innocent victim, who did nothing to deserve such treatment. But when a civilian tangles with a cop, nine times out of ten the jury would hear evidence of contemporaneous and/or prior conduct by the victim that is less than exemplary. From such conduct grows "reasonable doubt." As a matter of fairness, this should not have mattered, if the police behavior violated the law. But attorneys—certainly prosecutors—learn early on that fairness has little to do with the day-to-day world of the law.

For young prosecutors looking to build up an impressive win-loss record, police brutality cases were not the way to go. These matters seldom were resolved by plea bargain—most officers were willing to take their chances with a jury, rather than risk any blemish on their records that might be a bar to career advancement. Criminal Section prosecutors had been on a losing streak, and our bosses were not happy about it. With the national mood running conservative and the economy not doing well, convicting cops was not high on any juror's priority list. Still, we had little choice but to push these cases—they were almost always ignored by local and state authorities, and we could not let bad apples in law enforcement believe that they were utterly immune from accountability.

∼

Of all the places where deterrence against police brutality and official misconduct was needed, Louisiana was probably the most egregious. The New Orleans Police Department, according to Justice Department data, was the most corrupt and brutal metropolitan police force in the country (edging out Houston, where I also put in my fair share of time). Law enforcement officers in southern Louisiana were poorly paid, not well-educated, and often moonlighted at second jobs of dubious reputation. Police misconduct in New Orleans and the surrounding parishes often went well beyond the mere "physically overzealous," into areas such as suffocation and other forms of torture; murder-for-hire; and a dazzlingly-inventive smorgasbord of graft and extortion.

Various components of the Department of Justice were kept busy trying to put at least some fear of God into this cesspool of official lawlessness, but only the occasional prosecution was successful. The state's tradition of official corruption was legendary. During my time in the Eastern District of Louisiana, I had to lobby hard for grand jury time, as a non-stop parade of state and local officials were brought into the federal courthouse almost as a rite of passage. One day in those halls of justice, I noticed a local celebrity holding court in the hallway. It was none other than Billy Cannon, legendary Louisiana State football icon and Heisman Trophy winner, under indictment (and eventually convicted and incarcerated) for counterfeiting. Some officials, like former governor Edwin Edwards, used their corruption as badges of honor in political campaigns. Edwards' slogan in a subsequent, successful, return to the governor's mansion was "Vote For The Crook." To be fair, his opponent was state legislator David Duke, Ku Klux Klan leader and purveyor of Nazi literature and memorabilia. It was all relative down in bayou country. But Governor Edwards eventually served his hard-earned time behind bars after all.

A brutally hot and muggy August day in St. Tammany Parish, Louisiana, 24 miles by causeway across Lake Pontchartrain from New Orleans. This was country in transition from backwoods to New South. Small businesses, schools, and roads were springing up to serve residents fleeing the Big Easy for more leg-room, but there were still plenty of gun shops and bait-and-tackle outlets, and more than the occasional alligator showed up in someone's backyard. St. Tammany Parish was home to Mandeville, the mental institution to which Blanche DuBois was led peacefully away in "A Streetcar Named Desire." Local color was everywhere in the Pelican State.

At Sunbelt Realty, a new business in a strip-mall on the main thoroughfare, office manager Lee Cunningham and two female associates were going through listings and making a few calls, hoping the struggling air conditioner could make it through the day without giving up. Drinking iced tea at a steady rate, the three realtors were relieved when a customer walked in—any break in the morning's languid routine was welcome. The visitor was George Kingston, a slightly-built African American wearing dark sunglasses, in need of a house to rent. After asking the appropriate questions to determine Kingston's particular needs, Cunningham handed him the keys to a small dwelling just across the blacktop parking lot.

As Kingston walked over to inspect the property, he was spotted by two policemen driving by in their cruiser. Seeing a black man approaching a house in this predominantly white neighborhood, Deputy Sheriff Wayne Chalfont decided that something must be amiss. He drove up to Kingston and confronted him. From that moment on, accounts, and lives, would be changed—but none for the better.

A year later, I was once again at my cluttered desk in my shabby Justice Department office, drowning in paper in the pre-computer age. I picked up a newly assigned case file—yet another police brutality matter from the Eastern District of Louisiana. A preliminary perusal indicated another classic "he said, he said" narrative. Here we go again, I figured: an innocent passer-by claims a cop "kicked my ass" for no reason whatsoever; the police officer states that the civilian was profane, uncooperative, and refused to explain why he was on the premises. The complainant suffered relatively minor injuries, and had a prior arrest record. This one looked like it would probably never even make it to grand jury, let alone trial, and this cop had as much chance of being convicted as I did of becoming Pope. In Greater New Orleans, incidents like this were as common as barking dog complaints. Hell, down there waterboarding was standard interrogation procedure long before Guantanamo. In the absence of an autopsy report, any prospective juror would regard this case as business as usual, nothing to get too upset about.

Kingston's and Chalfont's stories, as set forth in the F.B.I. interview reports in the file, turned out to be quite typical indeed for a police misconduct investigation. Kingston, single and living in New Orleans, was looking for a rental property closer to his place of employment as a security guard. He noted that Chalfont told him he'd received a radio report of a "suspicious black man" in the area, and accordingly accosted Kingston. After Kingston displayed his identification, Chalfont taunted him; unbuckled his firearm holster; and told Kingston "try me" when the latter persisted in asking why he was being braced. Kingston stated that he folded his arms, and that Chalfont then lashed him repeatedly across the face with old-style steel handcuffs. When Kingston tried to defend himself, Chalfont rammed his head into the patrol car; kicked him repeatedly; and finally handcuffed him and threw him into the back seat of the cruiser. Kingston reported that on the drive to the Sheriff's office, Chalfont told him "I'm going to get you." When Kingston complained to personnel at the Sheriff's Office, Chalfont yelled out "Get that black son of a bitch out of here."

Deputy Chalfont—measuring 6'2" and 243 pounds to Kingston's 5'7" and 170—reiterated his claim of a radio call to be on the lookout for a suspicious black male. He stressed Kingston's refusal to cooperate with a perfectly reasonable "stop and frisk," and that Kingston unleashed a stream of profanity for no reason. When he tried to handcuff Kingston, the latter charged him, at which point Chalfont realized he needed to call for back-up. He added that when he finally subdued Kingston, who continued to struggle and resist arrest, he found a knife on him, further justifying the police action.

The statement of Chalfont's partner, rookie Deputy Charles Montague, who was on one of his first patrols, caught my attention. The usual practice in these investigations was for partners to back each other up 100%, certainly for a rookie officer describing his veteran superior's actions, but Montague had been surprisingly noncommittal. He claimed to be busy calling in the deputies' location and running Kingston's driver's license, and therefore missed the physical confrontation. He did note that when he heard the commotion, Kingston appeared to be bleeding, but Montague added little else of consequence. Was his conscience troubling him, I wondered?

But what really stood out in the file were the accounts of the three realtors. A trio of white, suburban, neutral eye-witnesses—interviewed separately by the F.B.I.—gave statements that were thoroughly consistent in support of Kingston's account. Yvonne Beaupre, the youngest of the three office witnesses, said she had never seen anything like the unprovoked assault on Kingston, and yelled to office manager Cunningham, "Do something; they'll kill him!" Katherine Mills, a matronly, reserved woman, told the Bureau that Kingston demonstrated admirable restraint, keeping his hands folded while the Deputy taunted and struck him. Finally, Cunningham ran out of the office and told the officers, "God damn it, that's enough." All three told the deputies that it was the victim, not the officers, who needed back-up. Finally, the realtors telephoned the Sheriff's office after Kingston was driven away, to complain of his treatment and because they feared for his safety en route to the jail.

I had seldom—let's make that never—seen such unanimous eye-witness support for the victim in such an incident. Even more strikingly, these were—at least on paper—dream witnesses: completely neutral, they had no prior dealings with Kingston or the two deputies. All had squeaky-clean records—three white, middle class business people with no grudges against the police. To say that it was rare for such citizens to call in a police brutality complaint involving an unknown black victim would be a gross understatement.

Even in those cases where a victim's statement was supported by eye-witnesses, those witnesses tended to fall into one of several, usually fatal categories: friends or associates of the victim; owners of criminal records; known to be hostile to law enforcement; under the influence of alcohol or drugs; inarticulate, vision-impaired, or otherwise flawed as trial witnesses; or, fearful of testifying.

But Cunningham, Beaupre and Mills came with none of these detriments. They seemed like classic good Samaritans, so outraged by what they had seen that they took it upon themselves to complain to the authorities. And, for the icing on the cake from a prosecutor's perspective, they viewed the entire proceedings through a clear, plate-glass window at a short distance, in broad daylight on a sun-drenched day. I couldn't let this one go by. Louisiana, here I come.

The next step was to present this matter to a federal grand jury in New Orleans, with the goal of securing an indictment against Chalfont for a criminal civil rights violation. The grand jury—comprised of twenty-three residents of the Eastern District of Louisiana—would hear a summary of the case; view physical evidence and official documents (primarily St. Tammany Sheriff's Department incident reports); and listen to testimony from key parties. We wanted to move quickly. This was not an extremely complicated case, and we wanted the testimony of the victim and eye-witnesses on record before anyone might have a change of heart. You just never knew in these cases: witnesses could be intimidated or silenced for all sorts of reason, legal and illegal. Everyone had their vulnerabilities and pressure points. We knew from considerable experience that Louisiana lawmen were not exactly beholden to a strict code of ethics.

Kingston himself, a hapless soul with a history of periodic brushes with the law (fortunately, no convictions), repeated relocations throughout the South and Southwest, and a less than stellar employment history, was a potential candidate to fall off our radar screen. Hardly likely to settle down permanently in St. Tammany Parish after what he had been through, we needed to keep him happy and in our sights until the trial was over. Among the wide variety of telephone calls a federal prosecutor doesn't want to make from the road back to the home office, the one that began with the phrase "my key witness is missing" ranked near the top.

Pursuant to standard federal practice, the potential defendant, or "target," was issued a letter of invitation to testify before the grand jury.

Deputy Chalfont, like most targets, declined on the advice of counsel, rather than risk incriminating himself under oath (his attorney, under federal law, would not be permitted in the grand jury room). The documentary evidence reviewed by the grand jurors was generally favorable to the government. Among other things, both the complaint of a "suspicious black male" and the knife allegedly found on Kingston proved to be figments of Deputy Chalfont's imagination. Thank you, St. Tammany Parish Sheriff's Office, for your extremely thorough police reports. These reports, and all evidence in the custody of the Sheriff's Department, were subpoenaed by the prosecution as soon as the grand jury was impaneled—such documents sometimes had a remarkable way of disappearing, never to be rediscovered.

Of the three realtor-witnesses, we decided to subpoena Cunningham and Mills before the grand jury. Yvonne Beaupre had moved to Texas since the incident; we would definitely need her at trial, but we chose not to inconvenience her twice when her testimony was so similar to that of her colleagues. Neither Cunningham nor Mills required extensive preparation. Their testimony remained consistent; unlike many witnesses in criminal proceedings, they seemed comfortable, even eager to tell their stories. Their demeanor and background could not have been more suitable for the quintessentially middle class members of the grand jury.

By contrast, as in so many police brutality cases, the toughest nut to crack was the victim. Kingston was reluctant, depressed, and scared. And who could blame him? This was a criminal case, United States versus Chalfont, should the grand jury choose to indict. Even if his assailant were convicted, there was really nothing in it for poor Kingston. He would have to relive his nightmare both in the grand jury and at a public trial; be subpoenaed away from his job several times; and be subjected to a humiliating, no-holds-barred cross-examination, for which no amount of preparation would give him sufficient confidence for the ordeal that lay ahead of him.

At our preparation sessions, Kingston proved to be quite quick on the uptake, possessing the savvy that those lacking formal education and connections often acquire in order to survive in a world stacked against them. He understood that we needed him for the greater good of enforcing civil rights. But at this point, he was just tired of it all, beaten down, and ready to move on to the next chapter in a dispiriting life's journey. He wanted to get out of Dodge, leave St. Tammany Parish and Louisiana behind, and see how things might work out for him in Mississippi.

Good God, I thought: what a depressing commentary on the plight of a black man in mid-20th Century America: Mississippi was his idea of the land of opportunity! Since the confrontation at Sunbelt Realty, Kingston had broken up with his girlfriend; his employment as a security guard was hanging by a thread; and he was on medication for both physical and emotional ailments resulting from his arrest. He wore sunglasses at all times; when he did briefly remove them, he avoided eye contact. He was perfectly articulate when he chose to be, but he made it quite clear that if subpoenaed to testify, he would not do so happily, and repeatedly urged me to drop the whole damn thing.

Unwisely relaying this state of affairs to my section chief back in

Washington, I got the earful I should have expected. I'm pretty sure that smoke was coming out of the receiver on my end. I should know damn well by now that the victims in these cases were not pillars of the community; of course they were scared and depressed; every one of them wanted to put this unpleasantness behind them and get on with their lives. No one ever said this would be easy. This is what we pay you for. I was ordered to do whatever it took, no matter how much time might be necessary, to prepare Kingston for grand jury and trial.

In the grand jury, where there was no cross-examination, and the standard for indictment was probable cause, rather than guilt beyond a reasonable doubt, Kingston proved to be Good Enough For Government. The grand jurors returned the following, fairly typical federal indictment:

UNITED STATES OF AMERICA

v.

WAYNE B. CHALFONT

The Grand jury charges: that in St. Tammany Parish, Louisiana, within the Eastern District of Louisiana, WAYNE B. CHALFONT, then a St. Tammany Parish Deputy Sheriff, while acting under color of the laws of the State of Louisiana, did willfully strike and assault George G. Kingston, then an inhabitant of the State of Louisiana, and did thereby willfully deprive George G. Kingston of the right secured and protected by the Constitution and laws of the United States not to be deprived of liberty without due process of law. In violation of Title 18, United States Code, Section 242.

∼

We were fortunate to get a swift trial date, and I decamped back to the Big Easy for the duration. There were worse locales for government travel—in fact, for a music fanatic like me, there were none better. The pressure-packed preparation for trial—where, in contrast to the grand jury, there would be no margin for error—would be mitigated by the sensual atmosphere of my adopted favorite among American cities. Having grown up in San Francisco, my standards were pretty high, but I had never experienced anything like New Orleans. All the music I'd always played and loved was within easy reach; there were succulent dishes to kill for; Mardi Gras and all its bizarre offshoots in full swing; and all were eminently affordable in a Deep South economy. Record stores (before they went the way of the dinosaur) were stocked with LPs that I could never find up North; the streets were full of musicians playing for tips who would be first-call aces back home. It was an exotic blend of cultures absolutely unique in the white-bread southland: Creole, Cajun, Spanish, French, American Indian, Italian, African, Caribbean. Voodoo was a mainstream religion, and there was no such thing as closing time. Eyes on the prize, Brother Feinstein: there's work to be done.

My local counterpart, Assistant United States Attorney Tom Watson, was an ambitious, young, politically connected, conservative Republican from Mississippi. We couldn't possibly have had less in common. He was a very busy man in this prosecutor's heaven, but he found the time to give me the logistical assistance and inside knowledge that I always needed on the road. He acted as "second chair," providing an invaluable local presence in the highly insular Louisiana legal world. Louisiana's legal system, alone in the United States, was (and is) based not on the English common law that we all studied in law school, but rather on the French Code Napoleon. Almost all the local attorneys went to Louisiana State or Tulane Law Schools, and it seemed as though they all knew and played golf with each other. There were unwritten customs and traditions that I could never grasp, and Watson did a fine job of helping me navigate them. In other words, he ran interference for me by on the many occasions when I threatened to make a fool of myself.

The presiding judge, Charles Schwartz, was refreshingly informal and courteous to an outsider (qualities I had not often encountered in the federal judiciary), a true bon vivant who loved his New Orleans cuisine. In classic Big Easy fashion, the judge took lengthy lunch breaks for meals at a succession of his favorite establishments, letting us know where he could be contacted in case of emergency. He generally gave the prosecution a fair shake in his pretrial rulings, but he could not hide his view that what we had here was essentially much ado about nothing, a minor incident that did not rise to the level of a federal civil rights case. I

repeatedly stressed that this entire matter was unnecessarily instigated by the racial bias of the defendant, whose conduct was so egregious that it was the subject of an official complaint by three neutral (hint, Your Honor: "white") eye-witnesses. But Judge Schwartz, like so many others I encountered in these cases, saw it as a waste of federal tax dollars. Ultimately I was able to finesse his views, as he was fairly careful to refrain from expressing them in front of the jury.

My opposing counsel, Julian Rodrigue, from a venerable Louisiana legal family, was courtly and hospitable, doing what he could to make a carpetbagger like yours truly feel relatively comfortable on foreign turf.

The trial was predictably contentious, but, in contrast to what was fast becoming the norm north of the Mason-Dixon Line, the hostilities were left behind in the courtroom, and the attorneys treated each other as brethren at the bar during recesses. In fact, during jury deliberations—as tense a time imaginable in criminal proceedings—Rodrigue pointed me in the right direction for that most essential of New Orleans survival tools: a fine meal right around the corner from the courthouse.

I had hoped that, for a change, we might end up with a vaguely diverse jury for this trial, given the high minority population in the judicial district. I had even heard talk that black citizens had finally started being admitted to the voter rolls in significant numbers, thus qualifying them for jury panels. However, I had no such luck: the jury pool was overwhelmingly white, and the defense, as was their prerogative, excused most all of the minorities in the jury box. We ended up with one African-American juror, and she was the mother of a New Orleans police officer. Mama said there'd be days like this.

At trial, we decided to lead off with Kingston. We had promised him that we would do what we could to minimize his waiting time in a hot, uncomfortable witness room, while his nervousness and fear grew. This also gave the jury an opportunity right out of the gate to compare Kingston's slight build with the hulking figure of Chalfont, sitting nearby at the defense table. In a criminal trial, what a juror sees is at least, if not more, important than what he or she hears. Accordingly, we had Kingston identify the large, sharp steel handcuffs with which he was repeatedly struck. These were then passed around in the jury box. Kingston was clearly uncomfortable, but he stuck to his story, on both direct and cross-examination, in all material respects. He became emotional when again recounting his experience, and lashed out a bit at Rodrigue. But that was all right. Emotion and discomfort under these circumstances are not going to shock most jurors. What a trial attorney lived in fear of was a witness who reacted to the inevitable pressure by changing his story, or making things up in the vain hopes of pleasing the jury. Losing composure might be embarrassing, but losing credibility meant disaster.

I breathed a sigh of relief when Kingston stepped down from the stand. We had confidence in our three eye-witnesses, and we were not disappointed. We put them on consecutively, to give the jurors a steady drumbeat of witnesses who were not only consistent with each other, but with Kingston's initial account. Sometimes, this could be tricky. If the jury heard basically identical testimony too many times, there was a danger that they might find it rehearsed or manufactured. This time, sincere disgust with the defendant's conduct came through in the emotional quality displayed by each witness. When Cunningham told of finally running outside and yelling "God damn it, that's enough" to a deputy sheriff, it definitely rang true. When the demure Katherine Mills testified that she never dreamed that she would one day file a police brutality complaint, it came through as the personification of the Good Citizen who simply had to do the right thing.

Finally, there was Yvonne Beaupre, who had been given a pass for the grand jury. No two ways about it, she was a bombshell in the courtroom. To say that she had a voluptuous figure would be putting it mildly, and her bright gold, form-fitting knit dress was working overtime to contain it. We had, of course, given her the standard pretrial instruction to dress "conservatively," but this proved to be a relative term in New Orleans at the height of Mardi Gras season, where masks, tiaras, and the occasional whip are not uncommon. She had long, wavy red hair cascading almost to her waist, and a syrupy drawl reminiscent of Scarlet O'Hara. One of a trial attorney's many courtroom tasks was to be sure that the jury's attention was focused on the witness at critical times; that was unnecessary for Yvonne Beaupre. The jury took in her every word and move, and she corroborated her former Sunbelt Realty colleagues to a T.

Besides Chalfont himself, the major defense witness was the wild card in the case, his partner Charles Montague. He gave the expected testimony regarding the defendant's good character, and general reputation as an excellent law enforcement officer. But Montague's prior statement that he had been busy on the police radio during most of the confrontation made it impossible for him to effectively exonerate Chalfont. Montague did state that his senior partner asked the realtors to call for back up, as required by standard police procedure. However, he did recall that office manager Cunningham then said that it was actually Kingston who needed the back-up. While adamantly testifying that Chalfont intended no harassment, and that it was a potentially dangerous situation, Montague eventually admitted that had he been in charge, he might have handled the incident differently.

Wayne Chalfont, well prepared and well-spoken, stuck close to his previous statements to the FBI and the sheriff's office. He stressed that he engaged in "stop and frisk" routines all the time, but that very few people had been as combative and uncooperative as Kingston. He vehemently denied having any racist views, and emphasized that he treated everyone alike, because "I'm not prejudiced."

By now I had heard this litany too many times, recently from Ku Klux Klan members before a Georgia grand jury, who characterized the KKK as a "social club" that did a lot of charity and other good works in the community. It was a good thing that my colleague Tom Watson would be cross-examining the defendant, because I could feel my blood pressure rising. This case seemed to be shaping up pretty well for us. What we didn't need was me getting on my high horse, playing John Brown in front of a Louisiana jury. Sure enough, Watson took the high road. He was cool as a cucumber, avoiding the potential tinder-box of the race card, instead concentrating on Chalfont's now discredited stories about the mysterious radio call regarding a suspicious black man and the nonexistent knife allegedly found on Kingston. This made for a nice finishing touch: the last thing the jurors heard was the defendant admitting to a series of falsehoods. In the courtroom, nothing was as disastrous, and as impossible to remedy, as credibility lost.

When the jury returned to deliver its verdict, I was still feeling fairly optimistic; we experienced no significant setbacks at trial, and our witnesses remained consistent. Still, as Watson cautioned me all along, juries didn't like to convict cops down here. When the bailiff handed the verdict form up to the bench, Judge Schwartz read it; rolled his eyes; and shook his head slightly. Guilty As Charged, and thank the Lord for the jury system.

Rodrigue, ever the gentleman, shook my hand in congratulations, and Watson and I exited the courtroom before exchanging a discreet, if not entirely professional, high-five. My colleague could not resist kidding me about my closing summation to the jury, during which I expressed regret over bringing charges against a brother law enforcement officer. "What was that bullshit all about?" he laughed.

But all was not happiness. Chalfont's sheriff's department colleagues, a constant but fairly restrained supporting presence throughout the trial, finally boiled over. There were hoots of displeasure, angry stomping, and muted obscenities in the hallways. I was told in no uncertain terms that I must have had better things to do than to come all the way down here to ruin a good man's career over a half-assed incident like this. Watson wisely whisked me away, where I answered, very carefully, some questions from the press. I was told by reporters and courthouse veterans that this was the first time a white police officer had been convicted of police brutality against a black victim in Louisiana. I didn't know whether that was true, but right after a victory, I wasn't above basking in a little glory.

But ultimately, I couldn't kid myself. The government prevailed in this case for one reason, and one reason only: because the victim's story was corroborated by three neutral, middle-class, white eyewitnesses. Without their confident, articulate testimony, I would have had my ass handed to me on a silver platter. What of the thousands of similar cases down through the years, up north as well as below the line, of race-based stop-and-frisks, verbal protests met with fists and clubs, and bogus arrests? Those almost always took place away from public view, with no chance of vindication for the victims. Yeah, we won this one and it felt damn good, but I got to play a strong hand.

Sentencing proved to be anticlimactic. Chalfont, of course, had no prior criminal record; the victim's injuries were far from life-threatening; and Judge Schwartz reiterated his belief that this did not amount to a civil rights violation, because the case lacked "racial overtones." At this comment, Watson gave me a look of pure poison, knowing that I could not be trusted with my emotions upon hearing such nonsense. I kept my mouth shut, but I felt like flinging the water pitcher on our counsel table toward the bench. Good God, man, does the defendant have to wear a robe and hood to get your attention? Didn't you hear the deputy admit under oath that he invented the police radio call about the "suspicious black man?"

But that was all water under the bridge. Chalfont was sentenced to the maximum one year imprisonment, suspended; three years probation; and one year of public service of twelve hours per month. Judge Schwartz rejected our recommendation that the defendant be severed from law enforcement, although neither he nor the St. Tammany's Sheriff's office has ever apologized to Kingston nor shown any remorse. On the contrary, Chalfont incurred no administrative discipline whatsoever; there wasn't even an internal investigation.

Afterward, I treated myself to a grand meal at the incomparable Commander's Palace, a highly unusual splurge on official travel for probably the best meal of my life to date. Farewells over, I took the venerable streetcar past the wildly-colorful blossoms, ancient oaks, and magnificent antebellum mansions of the Garden District back to my hotel, to pack up and make the usual mad dash for the airport and home. I would return to New Orleans and environs many times, sometimes for business, sometimes for pleasure, but I don't think I will ever really understand how a place of such joy tolerates such rot at its core.

Chalfont's appeal, citing, among other grounds, prosecutorial misconduct on my part (I was quite used to this claim by now), was unanimously rejected by the United States Court of Appeals. Judge Schwartz, who kept his opinions to himself when it counted, served on the federal bench until 2001, and passed away at age 90. Tom Watson went on to a distinguished career with the United Sates Attorney's Office in New Orleans. Sunbelt Realty's office in St. Tammany Parish closed in a declining housing market, its employees scattering to the winds. Large areas of St. Tammany Parish, like most of the low-lying land around Lake Pontchartrain, suffered terrible damage from Hurricanes Katrina and Rita in 2005.

Deputy Sheriff Wayne Chalfont, while temporarily enjoying the support of the parish sheriff and his fellow deputies, did not fare well following his trial. Few law enforcement officers will survive a federal criminal conviction unscathed, and Chalfont's descent was slow but sure. He eventually lost his deputy position and moved on to smaller police agencies. His marriage broke up, and he finally left law enforcement. At his last job, at a K-Mart in a neighboring parish, he sustained a serious injury, resulting in workers compensation litigation. At the age of forty-one, a broken man, he died of a drug overdose.

George Kingston, the star-crossed drifter, continued his eastward trek across the South in search of solace and security. After the jury's verdict, which brought a rare, brief smile to his face, we shook hands, vowing to stay in touch, but of course we never heard from one another again. I might win some cases, but I don't save lives. He declined a ride, walked down the courthouse steps, and turned right toward the ancient bus station. Once there, he removed his worldly goods from a storage locker and boarded the Greyhound into the night, disappearing once again into an America I would never know.

∽

Postscript: July 21, 2009.

Black Scholar's Arrest Raises Profiling Questions

Boston (AP): Supporters of a prominent Harvard University black scholar who was arrested at his own home by police responding to a report of a break-in say he is the victim of racial profiling. Henry Louis Gates, Jr. had forced his way through the front door of his home because it was jammed, his lawyer said Monday. By the times police arrived, Gates was already inside. Police say he refused to come outside to speak with an officer, who told him he was investigating a report of a break-in.

"Why, because I'm a black man in America?" Gates said. Gates said he turned over his driver's license and Harvard ID—both with his photos—and repeatedly asked for the name and badge number of the officer, who refused. He said he then followed the officer as he left his house onto his front porch, where he was handcuffed in front of other officers. He was arrested on a disorderly conduct charge after police said he exhibited loud and tumultuous behavior.

And just as in the case of George Kingston, one of so many earlier participants in this timeless dance, all charges against Professor Gates were dropped.

Howard L. Feinstein

Fire on the Bayou

Knights in White Satin

Several years had passed, but I was still smarting from the jury's "not guilty" verdict in the Willacoochee Ku Klux Klan case in South Georgia. I had certainly been busy in the meantime, running down and prosecuting cross-burners, murderous police officers, racist individuals and public officials, and other assorted malefactors. But I wanted another crack at a Klan reign of terror in the worst way. This drive for revenge or redemption—whatever one might choose to call it—would not be found in any prosecutor's handbook, certainly not at the tradition-bound U.S. Department of Justice. A prosecutor, as the Canons of Ethics instructed us, was a representative of the public, who at all times must keep the goal of even-handed justice in mind.

We were supposed to prosecute "the crime, not the person." But I was made of flesh and blood. I wasn't some robot enforcing particular federal laws that happened to fit within my job description. If it were just a simple matter of enforcing the criminal laws, I could work for a District Attorney or a U.S. Attorney's Office, and go after drug dealers, bank fraud artists, or Wall Street swindlers, which I did during a subsequent phase of my career. But in my younger days, what got my blood circulating early in the morning was the prospect of doing battle with defendants whom I saw as the ultimate evil on the battleground of civil rights. I needed to believe that while the case at hand might nominally be United States vs. John Doe, it was really Feinstein vs. Satan. For me, this was the only way to stoke the "fire in the belly" that our superiors demanded of us. If that made me some kind of zealot, then I plead guilty.

As it always did, one day the great Wheel of Justice stopped on my number, and a thick batch of FBI reports fastened with string was dropped onto my desk like the morning paper, minus the dew. They told a sordid tale of typical Ku Klux Klan terror, aimed at the classic Klan target of interracial couples. There were robed and hooded visits to residences in the middle of the night; crudely threatening letters and leaflets; boycotts of businesses which fail to sympathize with the KKK world-view; the procuring of weapons to shoot up a radio station; and additional acts of hatred, all in the usual sleepy southern locale, now paralyzed with fear. All this sounded very much like the Willacoochee case, complete with the classic Klan target of interracial relationships. This looked like something I could really sink my teeth into, but there was one major problem: in the bureaucratic language of the FBI, this was an "UNSUB" file, meaning that no targets have been identified. And no targets meant no defendants; therefore, no prosecution. But the FBI Headquarters civil rights unit across the street was on the case; I let them know that this matter appeared to satisfy the legal requirements for a grand jury investigation, and that no efforts in the field should be spared. As long as the statute of limitations (in this case, the standard five years for a federal prosecution) had not expired, we would keep this one on our radar screen. Sure enough, a few months later, the monthly FBI report was no longer captioned "UNSUB"; instead, it bore the names of my newest nemesis, one Marshall Lanier—an Oakdale, Louisiana Klansman—and his faithful comrades.

The principal targets of this latest Klan campaign were the owners of an Oakdale nursing home, Ray (white male) and Carolyn (black female) Sievers. As an interracial couple, they were every Klansman's nightmare in the crusade against race-mixing. Carolyn served as day-to-day administrator of the nursing home, while Ray spent considerable time managing KREH, a local radio station. Lanier, a rising star in the KKK galaxy, had been identified by the FBI, through matching fingerprints and typewriter and stationery samples, as the ringleader in this effort to keep the races apart and in their proper places. His aides-de-camp were, for the most part, fellow soldiers stationed at nearby Fort Polk. Lanier, in addition to his position with the Klan, was said to have a record including previous racially motivated crime.

On paper, this shaped up as a promising case.

But as the Willacoochee case had painfully taught me, Klan prosecutions, like football games, were played in the real world, not on paper. For the jurors in the Southern District of Georgia, overwhelming fingerprint evidence and an undeniable record of racist views on the part of the defendant were not enough. I had to assume that this same situation would exist in the Western District of Louisiana, where once again the jury figured to be a whiter shade of pale. This time, I would need to obtain considerably more, and much stronger, evidence. Once again I packed my bags for a long stay Below The Line, telling myself that if I came back empty-handed from this battle, perhaps I wasn't cut out for this life. On the other hand, I was headed for Louisiana, my southern oasis, where at least I could count on some good music and food.

⌒

Alas, Oakdale proved to be very much of the Other Louisiana. No Creole belles or Mardi Gras Indians. Piney woods and scorched prairie, instead of drooping Spanish moss and cypress trees on the bayous. Confederate memorials and main streets lined with evangelical churches, instead of the predominantly Catholic South Louisiana culture of pre-Lenten revelry, with its wine, women and song. Rev. Jimmy Swaggart and his similarly fire-and-brimstone cousin, Jerry Lee Lewis, in place of the rollicking Bourbon Street fireworks of Fats Domino and Dr. John. This was hard-shell Baptist country (Catholics historically being one of the Klan's scapegoats), unmoderated by the cosmopolitan influences of the port of New Orleans. This was the Louisiana of DeRidder and Denham Springs, postmarks I recognized readily from KKK mass mailings and written threats.

I was headed down to the Louisiana of Galvez, birthplace of Imperial Wizard Bill Wilkinson, early mentor to Klansman and Nazi David Duke, both of them mentors to my Willacoochee foes and my new antagonists, Marshall Lanier and company. This was the Louisiana of the Colfax riot in 1873, when over 150 black citizens were slaughtered after surrendering, in the worst Reconstruction Era racial violence on record. And of Norco, site of the largest slave revolt in American history in 1811, after which 21 rebellion leaders were executed, their heads mounted on pikes along the River Road. And of Bogalusa, the quintessential blue-collar southern mill town, where, during the heyday of the civil rights movement in the 1960's, the Klan was so powerful that it spawned a rare armed black opposition group, the Deacons of Defense, a Dixie version of the Black Panther Party of my Bay Area youth.

The cover photograph from the 2005 state Calendar of Events, depicting a black man whirling a white woman around the dance floor in classic Louisiana "Let The Good Times Roll" fashion, was surely not taken in Oakdale. It was a dusty town of 8,000, just on the edge of the "Acadia Parishes", but totally lacking in their Cajun and Creole joie de vivre. Allen Parish was flat and wooded, lumber and saw mill country with a history of very few job opportunities. During this particular Klan campaign, unemployment in Allen Parish was a brutal 19.3%, the highest in the state. The Sievers residence, where hooded

Klansmen paid a nighttime visit, was listed as a "garden apartment." But I found nothing on the premises resembling a garden, just an expanse of sun-baked brown grass and weeds, littered with trash.

There was practically nothing to keep young people occupied, and precious few jobs that could even come close to supporting a family: a perfect breeding ground for the Ku Klux Klan and their ilk. Even the town's official historical brochure, on display at the Oakdale Branch of the Allen Parish Library, was devoid of positive attractions. While doing some background research on an early visit, I was particularly impressed by the following passage:

"This country has its share of vipers. There are several kinds. The large rattler; the ground rattler; and most feared, the moccasin; the copperhead; the coral…. There are many spiders and tarantulas. There are alligators in every stream."

Too bad I figured to be too busy to stop in at any real estate offices.

My task of compiling a convincing mass of evidence was aided immeasurably by a first-rate local team. Assistant U.S. Attorney Joe Jarzabek, an experienced, jovial Navy veteran who related effortlessly to the local citizenry, was based to the north in Shreveport, but he traveled to central Louisiana, including marathon grand jury sessions in Alexandria, without hesitation whenever he was needed. On the heels of a run of rather lackluster FBI case agents, I was blessed with the presence of Ken Roberson, a bureau veteran who was finishing up his career in the Monroe, Louisiana office, just over the state line from his native Arkansas. If there was anyone in the state with a wider network of sources and local knowledge, I didn't know who it would be, because this guy obviously knew everything and everyone.

In addition to his tireless work on the case at hand, Roberson occasionally highlighted our endless drives through Oakdale and the surrounding area by pointing out various houses and places of business, providing a colorful rundown on the criminal and other questionable activities of various residents and proprietors. This was crucial intelligence that I, even if I had a spare millennium, could not possibly obtain. When the rubber hit the road, and we needed to persuade people to cooperate before the grand jury, those personal insights would prove to be absolutely critical.

I soon learned that Jarzabek and Roberson formed a legendary team in those parts, with a track record of doing whatever was necessary to bring those who ran afoul of federal criminal law to justice. Their strengths complemented one another perfectly. They had developed a rhythm, like a finely-tuned basketball squad, which would entice and trap many an unwary perpetrator. I had as strong a local team as I could hope for; if things didn't go well, I would have no one to blame but myself.

It was Roberson who had developed the key fingerprint and typewriter evidence tying Lanier to the threatening communications, and the grand jurors were suitably impressed. But we would need live witnesses to nail this case down, and that required plenty of legwork. Through many days of hushed conversations and confrontational interviews, running down a steady stream of leads, tips, and rumors, we ultimately identified several key individuals, whom we hoped would aid us in casting a net around Marshall Lanier, the big fish:

Three Oakdale merchants who told the grand jurors that they had been so scared of the KKK threats that they withdrew advertising from KREH, the radio station that employed Ray Sievers; Andy McCutcheon, a soldier in Lanier's unit at Ft. Polk who accompanied him on the nighttime visit in Klan garb to the Sievers' home; George Bergeron, another soldier who helped distribute the threatening KKK stickers and leaflets; and, Marvin Tinsley, an Oakdale resident who Lanier recruited, and furnished with a .22 rifle, for the purpose of shooting up the KREH signal tower.

Fortunately, the military was readily cooperative in identifying the key perpetrators, including the tedious process of tracking down their whereabouts since their time at Fort Polk. Throughout my civil rights career, the armed forces generally took a strong stand against racial discrimination and harassment. The military, which didn't automatically spring to mind when one thought of civil rights enforcement, was actually in the forefront of the battle against segregation and prejudice, compared with most governmental authorities.

One of the critical steps in preparing for a grand jury presentation was the high-stakes processing of deciding who to indict and who to immunize. It never felt good to give a "get out of jail free" card to persons associated with illegal conduct, but we had all learned the hard way that these cases were rarely won with innocent witnesses of exemplary character. Given that Bergeron did not participate in the nighttime visit, and Tinsley had backed out of the agreement to shoot up the signal tower, they were granted immunity, in exchange for very damning grand jury testimony against Lanier.

Andy McCutcheon was another story. He was involved in the frightening intrusion onto the Sievers property as well as the distribution of the threatening written material; we just could not justify giving him a free pass. After a lengthy, often tearful bargaining session, he agreed to plead guilty to one misdemeanor count. McCutcheon, an extremely unsophisticated farm boy from rural Michigan, was also the subject of a heated telephone conversation with my section chief back in Washington, who wanted me to put a body wire on McCutcheon to obtain incriminating evidence against Lanier. But McCutcheon was so hapless that he had recently become confused and missed his flight in the tiny Alexandria, Louisiana airport, a feat akin to getting lost in one's own home. To call him naïve and inarticulate was a gross understatement. I could not imagine a more disastrous candidate for undergoing the pressure-cooker of wearing a wire. For the only time I could recall in my long history of arguments with my superiors back home, my view prevailed.

Lanier, like most federal jury targets, declined to testify. But his racist background was read into the record by case agent Roberson. While in his twenties, this Oakdale native had constructed a bomb, using gunpowder, firecrackers, nails, staples, and other missiles; tied it to a string with a dollar bill at the other end, and placed it next to a railroad track adjacent to an area used as a playground by local black children. One child blessedly reported the bomb to police without touching it, and the device was dismantled by a bomb squad from Fort Polk, where Lanier would one day organize his Ku Klux Klan chapter. He was charged with four criminal violations, and pled guilty.

Normally, a prior conviction for a crime with such a strikingly similar motive would be worth its weight in gold to a prosecutor. However, we could not be confident that a trial jury would ever learn of this horrific act. Five years after his guilty plea, Lanier received a full pardon from the governor of Louisiana, none other than Edwin Edwards, who had campaigned as the racial liberal against the notorious David Duke in the 1991 gubernatorial election. And five years after that pardon, Lanier's record was ordered expunged, with the full concurrence of the Allen Parish District Attorney. I was a long way from home, but if this was what passed for Louisiana justice, I was indeed a stranger in a strange land.

We also acquired an additional, extremely helpful compilation of evidence that we were able to put before the grand jurors. Pursuant to their plea agreements and grants of immunity, Lanier's confederates were under a continuing obligation to furnish us with any useful evidence that came their way. It turned out that Lanier continued to advise his old army buddies throughout our investigation, and these words of wisdom were handwritten, signed, and deposited in the United States mails:

Letter from Marshall Lanier to George Bergeron:

> "I wanted to let you know that my father died. This should make them hesitant to indict me. I strongly believe once they are told of this that when they vote, they will vote not to indict...I know you'll come through for me."

Letter from Marshall Lanier to Andy McCutcheon:

"*The man who was checking around here on the nigger-white situation told someone all they have is hearsay. But I still wouldn't ever write or speak about anything. The only way this case can be brought before a grand jury is if they come up with new significant evidence. This is impossible if the people involved don't talk...Silence is golden. Please watch what you say.*"

Usually, the atmosphere in a grand jury room tended to be anything but light-hearted. But the twenty-three assembled citizens got quite a laugh out of this sage correspondence.

༄

The grand jury, meeting in Alexandria, unanimously returned a four-count indictment against Lanier. Count One, outlining the overall conspiracy, read as follows:

UNITED STATES OF AMERICA

v.

MARSHALL C. LANIER

The Grand Jury Charges: In and around Oakdale, Louisiana, within the Western District of Louisiana, defendant MARSHALL C. LANIER, together with other persons known to the Grand Jury, did willfully conspire to oppress, threaten, and intimidate Ray Sievers, a citizen of the United States, in the free exercise and enjoyment of the rights and privileges secured to him by the Constitution and law of the United States, namely the right to be employed by the Radio Station KREH in Oakdale, Louisiana, pursuant to an employment contract, without discrimination on the basis of his own race or color or the race or color of his wife, and the right to occupy a dwelling without intimidation or interference because of his own race or color or the race or color of his wife.

It was part of the plan and purpose of the conspiracy that defendant carry out a concerted campaign of intimidation and terror aimed at Ray Sievers, his wife, and Radio Station KREH—including the intimidation of local merchants who, as a result of defendant's campaign, withdrew previously purchased advertising time on Radio Station KREH—in order to bring about the termination of Ray Sievers' employment by Radio Station KREH, and to drive Ray Sievers and his wife out of Oakdale, Louisiana.

OVERT ACTS

The Grand Jury charges that, in furtherance of the conspiracy and to accomplish the objectives thereof, the defendant committed the following overt acts, among others, within the Western District of Louisiana:

1. In or around Oakdale, Louisiana, defendant MARSHALL C. LANIER went to the residence of Marvin Tinsley and offered Tinsley money to assist him in driving Ray Sievers from his job and driving him out of town by shooting up the signal tower of Radio Station KREH.

2. In or around Oakdale, Louisiana, defendant LANIER gave Marvin Tinsley a .22 caliber rifle to use in shooting up the signal tower.

3. In or around Oakdale, Louisiana, defendant LANIER drove with Marvin Tinsley to the signal tower and instructed him as to how the shooting should be carried out.

4. In or around Oakdale, Louisiana, defendant LANIER caused to be attached to an automobile owned by Ray Sievers and his wife—said automobile then being parked near Sievers' residence—a sticker bearing the words:

"The Knights Of The Ku Klux Klan Is Watching You."

5. In or around Oakdale, Louisiana, defendant LANIER and other persons known to the Grand Jury, wearing robes and hoods and carrying Ku Klux Klan literature, drove to the residence of Ray Sievers and knocked on his door.

6. In or around Oakdale, Louisiana, defendant LANIER threatened Ray Sievers at his residence by telling Sievers and his wife to leave town because they were setting a bad example.

7. In or around Oakdale, Louisiana, after defendant retreated from Ray Sievers' residence, he distributed Ku Klux Klan literature around the apartment complex and drove away in his car, still wearing Ku Klux Klan robes and hoods.

8. In or around Oakdale, Louisiana, defendant LANIER wrote and caused to be duplicated a handwritten leaflet containing the following words:

Boycott 'Radio KREH' Radio

The Radio Station of Shame!

Citizens of Oakdale, have you been in town lately & notice a white fat Slob from the North & his nigger wife walking around our town like they were normal & as if they were still up North!

This is the type of trash the mayor has hired to run his radio station! Our people & kids are subjected to having this garbage to live among us thanks to the mayor. Let us send the trash and the mayor a message! That the white people still have pride in themselves & our Southern culture. We ask 'KREH' not be listen to as long as Mowad has the misfit at KREH. Encourage your friends to listen to Alex or other radio stations & stop buying at stores that support KREH. Mixed couples must leave. Lets join together for...

9. Defendant LANIER caused copies of the foregoing leaflet to be distributed to residences and places of business in and around Oakdale, Louisiana.

All in violation of Title 18, United States Code, Section 241.

Once again, the prospect of interracial association, let alone marriage, proved just too much for the sensibilities of the Klan. As John Lee Maynes had observed in Willacoochee, there wasn't much one could do about being born white or black. But to attend school, teach, work, socialize—even, God forbid, marry—across racial lines: well, that was against the natural order of things, and it would never be tolerated.

∽

Following arraignment and the posting of bail, Lanier failed to appear for a pretrial hearing, never a good way to get the presiding judge on your side. A bench warrant was issued; Lanier was quickly apprehended; and his bail was increased. Shortly after this development, Roberson laughingly informed me by telephone that we would unfortunately have to drop the case for lack of jurisdiction, because Lanier had told the local media that he did not recognize the authority of the federal government to prosecute him. Wonderful. Apparently, this was going to be all-out war.

But only a week later, I received a phone call from Lanier's counsel, Brian Le Febvre, a young, politically active attorney who was careful to let me know that he by no means shared his client's views on race relations. I was utterly astonished to hear that Lanier was seriously considering a plea agreement. Regaining my composure, I told Le Febvre that we would insist that any guilty plea be to a felony count. This would ensure that the defendant served a prison sentence, and would signal to the public that the Justice Department took conduct like Lanier's very seriously. Le Febvre responded that he would relay our position to his client, hoped to get back to me soon.

I'd been through this dance before, and had learned that it was definitely best to strike while the irons were hot. I had absolutely no idea what had prompted this new posture on the part of a racial sociopath like Lanier, but I was a prosecutor, not a psychiatrist, and I was long past concerning myself with the mysterious ways of human motivation. At this point, it was all about putting a win, not a loss, up on the scoreboard. As any experienced prosecutor knew well, a guilty plea was just as much of a conviction as a jury verdict, and it was imperative to grab it while it was still on the table.

I raced back to Louisiana, where we tediously hammered out an agreement requiring Lanier to plead to the felony civil rights conspiracy charge, with sentencing to be left to the discretion of the judge. No plea agreement became binding until it was finalized in court under oath, and Assistant United States Attorney Jarzabek, bless his heart, used his contacts and charm to arrange for the quickest sentencing date I had ever had. I wasn't about to let this one get away.

In Lake Charles, near the Texas border, the deal was done. A humbled Lanier admitted his deeds in open court, and District Judge Earl Veron sentenced him to three years confinement, to be served at Big Spring, Texas Federal Prison. Judge Veron delivered an impressive speech on the evils of these despicable hate crimes; pounded his gavel one final time; and Lanier was escorted from the courtroom in the custody of the bailiff.

What caused this true believer to throw in the towel: A religious conversion? A sudden flash of guilt? A weariness with the Ku Klux Klan lifestyle? A convincing lecture from his attorney on the odds stacked against him if he went to trial? I had no clue. Such speculation lay well beyond the scope of both my responsibility and my abilities. I prosecuted these people; I didn't analyze them. As brother Tennyson once wrote, ours is not to reason why, ours is but to do and die.

Jarzabek, Roberson and I, exhausted from travel and lack of sleep, walked down the street from the federal building in Lake Charles to a French Cajun restaurant for our obligatory celebration. Frog's legs, boudin, and other regional delicacies were washed down with beer. We all had been living with this case for one hell of a long time, and it had turned out nicely. After the meal, the waitress presented me—obviously the outsider of the group—with a certificate designating me as an "Honorary Coonass." Roberson and Jarzabek laughed hysterically at my embarrassment, and assured me that this was in fact an affectionate, perfectly acceptable term for "Cajun." Gentlemen, I thought, you can keep telling me that for the next ten hours, but somehow I don't think I'm ever going to feel comfortable with it. And anyway, Coonass just doesn't seem to go all that well with Feinstein.

Marshall Lanier served his federal time and apparently succeeded in staying on the right side of the law. He settled down to run a small business and raise a family in Central Louisiana. Ray and Carolyn Sievers, understandably, sold their nursing home, and relocated to the New Orleans area. Earl Veron served as senior District Judge until his death in 1990. Joe Jarzabek is still fighting the good fight as senior litigation counsel with the United States Attorney's Office in Shreveport. Sadly, Special Agent Ken Roberson passed away well before his time. He is remembered fondly within the Bureau, a dedicated public servant if there ever was one.

It would be nice to report that Oakdale became a place of racial harmony and civic progress, but that proved to be not quite the case. But a return visit in the wake of the devastation of Hurricanes Katrina and Rita did indicate some initial, positive developments. A meal just off the highway exit at the local McDonald's revealed black and white residents dining together, something I certainly wouldn't have seen back in the day. At the library in Oakdale, a black librarian was supervising both black and white workers, which would have been something out of a science fiction film during my previous time in this country.

I also observed more auto traffic and general bustle than I had remembered. I was told that this was due to the establishment of Oakdale's largest employer: a federal prison complex on a hundred acres of land. This was the lodestone story of post-industrial America: when times are hard and all else fails, there is always our biggest growth industry. Given the desperate employment history of Allen Parish, the prison must have seemed like manna from heaven.

People in town, both black and white, told me to talk to Wiley Shaw, founder and pastor of the Bread of Life Christian Center, and all-around community stalwart, for a frank appraisal of Oakdale yesterday and today. Reverend Shaw graciously made time for me on short notice, and I indeed learned a lot. He told me that the scenes I had observed of black and white residents dining and working together were a surface impression only. He recalled a recent incident involving two black friends dining together at a restaurant. One saw a white co-worker walk in and invited him to join the seated pair. The white customer did so, but that night he telephoned his colleague, telling him: "Don't you ever put me in that position again."

Reverend Shaw had lived nearly his whole life in Oakdale, and he had seen a lot. He raised the money for the handsome, modern church himself, from a black community hardly overflowing with wealth. He and his parishioners built the church with their bare hands. It was not only a place of worship, but a willing refuge for every individual, organization, and cause in the community. As in the general church community throughout the south and the nation, Sunday morning was a highly-segregated time in Oakdale, although Bread of Life Christian Center did have white members.

"Black and white must learn to respect each other," said Reverend Shaw; "God made us all. We're all human." He despaired of the scourge of drugs that was debilitating the black community. He was a tireless source of help to youth caught up in the criminal justice system, but noted that the high-level dealers, who were predominantly white, never seemed to be apprehended. And in a town as small and close-knit as Oakdale, everyone knew who they were.

Shaw was a self-made man, a veteran without higher education, possessed of a powerful work ethic and sense of community purpose. Growing up in the Jim Crow Deep South, he recalled the early days of school integration, when teachers referred to he and his classmates as "niggers." When he returned from his overseas tours of duty with the Army, he was determined to never again be treated as a second-class citizen. He was not completely without hope for the future, stating that the youth of the current generation were considerably more tolerant of diversity. However, he told me with more than a touch of wistfulness, "The black people here have heard so many insults and labels, and such low expectations, that we buy into them."

And doesn't that say it all. The Ku Klux Klan may march a lot less often these days, and registering to vote may no longer require an act of courage. But America's original sins of slavery and discrimination, and their sad legacy, have not yet been washed away. That task likely lies outside the realm of the law—certainly beyond my limited power.

Howard L. Feinstein

Fire on the Bayou

The Unforgiven

Early one morning over breakfast, I looked up from a newspaper article concerning community activists in the Washington, D.C. neighborhood where my wife directs a family social services program. One is described as a "civil rights worker." My wife paused and asks, "What does a civil rights worker do these days?" For once, I had no answer. Was this what it all had come to? The movement that had been the linchpin of so many lives was now a vaguely familiar, fast-fading concept—a relic of another era. This was not the first time I'd been reminded what creatures of the past my brethren and I had become; the riveting history we had lived through and played some small part in seemed utterly foreign to younger generations. A few years ago, at the beginning of the semester at the University of Maryland, I showed my undergraduate class in Current Issues in Civil Rights a video of early civil rights demonstrations from the acclaimed series "Eyes On The Prize." When I asked for questions or comments, an African American student raised her hand and exclaimed, "I can't believe they actually had separate sections of the buses for blacks and whites!"

She was no visitor from outer space. This was a well-educated college student from the national capital area in the 21st century. But I might as well have been discussing the age of the dinosaurs; we were not coming from the same worlds. It was time to revise the syllabus and start over at square one.

↬

I must be hopelessly naïve, because I am continually surprised when I am met with blank stares or yawns of boredom when I discuss the civil rights movement and its legacy. To me and others of a certain age, it not only was the most compelling and memorable event of our lives, but it truly represented America's Finest Hour. It is to America what the repulsion of the German invasion was to Britain in 1940, and what the 1789 overthrow of the monarchy was to France. As a longtime student and teacher of history, I don't make that claim lightly. But please: don't tell me about the colonists casting off British rule; don't tell me about the Civil War; don't tell me about the Allies' triumph over Germany and Japan; don't tell me about the first astronauts on the moon. No, the civil rights movement and the end of legal segregation was the closest that our young republic had come to demonstrating that we were serious about the founding promise of equality for all citizens. If Lincoln's address at Gettysburg marked the rebirth of a nation, the ascendancy of Jim Crow after Reconstruction necessitated a Third American Revolution, which didn't arrive until the people rose up en masse in the 1960s, culminating in that decade's landmark federal civil rights legislation. That was when America was truly Born Again.

It has been many years since these momentous events, and my small role in them, but they still dominate my world-view. Perhaps this is because, unlike so many public issues, civil rights has always carried with it such a straightforward good vs. evil dynamic. Coming from the worlds of law and academia, I am trained to see many different points of view, and to always respect the person even if I disagree with the proposition expressed. But when it comes to civil rights, racism, equal opportunity—call it what you may—I revert to my Old Testament judgmental nature. I will debate war and peace, foreign policy, the Middle East, the economy, health care, climate change, abortion, religion, or the Electoral College all day long. I will probably learn something, and not consider you an enemy. But when I hear anything approaching a discriminatory point of view, or if certain code words are spoken, my powers of reason vanish, and any semblance of respect for my colleague is forever gone.

But I am an anachronism. And the heroes and villains of the civil rights era, once household names, are inexorably passing on:

2005: Rosa Parks, whose simple "no" started it all in 1955 in Montgomery, Alabama. A tough-minded activist—nothing at all like the "tired working woman" of mythology—I was privileged to get to know her. She lived until the age of 92, still a champion of the cause.

2005: James Forman, whom I interviewed in California where he was speaking to raise funds for the continuing struggle in the South. He was an original Student Non-Violent Coordinating Committee pioneer who spoke truth to power, and would never, ever back down. His son, whom I also met, continues in a similar vein today.

2005: J.B. Stoner, the Georgia attorney who represented James Earl Ray, King's assassin. The ultimate segregationist true believer, he served time for church bombings, and bragged that he made Hitler look like a "racial moderate."

2006: Samuel Bowers, unrepentant Imperial Wizard of the Ku Klux Klan. He died in prison while serving a life sentence for the murder of civil rights worker Vernon Dahmer in Mississippi. He was also convicted for his part in the notorious Chaney, Goodman, and Schwerner murders.

2007: Oliver Hill of Virginia, at the age of 100. A key member of the fabled legal team assembled at Howard University Law School to fight segregation in the courts, including the historic Brown v. Board of Education litigation.

2007: Jim Clark, the veteran Dallas County, Alabama sheriff who led the "Bloody Sunday" attack on peaceful voting rights demonstrators at the Edmund Pettus Bridge in Selma in 1965. He was rarely seen in public without wearing a button concisely declaring "NEVER."

2008: Mildred Loving, the black woman from Virginia who had to leave the state to marry a white man. Her case went all the way to the U.S. Supreme Court, which finally outlawed anti-miscegenation laws in 1967. Her ordeal was on not a few minds several years ago, as I sat in the pews of a Virginia church to witness a similar union.

2009: James Bevel, the charismatic young minister who recruited college students and organized some of the earliest civil rights demonstrations, including the Nashville sit-ins protesting segregated public accommodations.

2009: J.L. Chestnut, the first African American lawyer in Selma, who headed the "Bloody Sunday" legal team. He represented Martin Luther King and other civil rights leaders on many occasions.

All are now gone, but they should not be forgotten.

It is not just that these historical figures are departing from the scene. The issues, the motivations, the key actors, the alliances—they all seem so different these days. By this time, I should not have been surprised when Nebraska's lone African-American state legislator successfully sponsored a bill to divide Omaha's public schools into three separate districts—one majority white, one black, one Hispanic. It is time, said State Senator Ernie Chambers, to "allow black educators to control schools in black areas." Indeed, the entire concept of public school desegregation has effectively been rendered obsolete, since the Supreme Court's decisions invalidating voluntary integration plans in Louisville and Seattle. And it has been quite a while since we have heard anything about the legislative or litigation efforts for "reparations," which would distribute funds to black communities as compensation for slavery.

And what of affirmative action, that always-controversial, barely-alive remnant of the civil rights age? In the wake of Ricci v. DeStefano, in which the Supreme Court overturned voluntary efforts by the city of New Haven to foster promotion of minority fire-fighters, if it is not dead, as characterized by the nonpareil civil rights chronicler Juan Williams, it is certainly on life support. Ricci also showed the changed nature of the line-up on the civil rights playing field, as the firefighter plaintiff class which challenged the affirmative action promotion plan included Hispanics. Writing for the Supreme Court majority in the 2003 decision upholding the University of Michigan Law School's minority-friendly admission policy, Justice Sandra O'Connor warned that within twenty-five years, affirmative action should no longer be necessary. Clearly the clock is ticking. To me, affirmative action seems a very small price to pay for four centuries of virulent discrimination. But perhaps it is time to focus on remedies that might benefit more people.

The ethnic make-up of the civil rights universe has indeed undergone a radical transformation. The anti-discrimination campaigns of the 1960s, as well as my own cases, featured real-life villains who now seem like obvious targets. But where are the Bull Connors, Lester Maddoxes, Louise Day Hickses, or Wayne Chalfonts of today? In my own national capital community, there is a tragic, never-ending parade of minority victims of violence, but one must look far and wide before finding a white perpetrator. In Washington, D.C. and neighboring Prince George's County, Maryland, the police departments, the boards of education, the corrections departments, and the other levers of government power, are firmly in minority hands, as is the case in urban jurisdictions nationwide. The victims are more often than not the same color as the "oppressors"—a far cry from the situation I encountered down South in the bad old days.

Long gone are the white power structure–Ku Klux Klan alliances like those we did battle with in Willacoochee. In fact, minority communities' most powerful current antagonist is probably Supreme Court Justice Clarence Thomas, justifying Thurgood Marshall's warning against naming just any African-American as his successor. No justice in recent memory has been as consistently hostile to civil rights enforcement as Thomas, a native of my old civil rights battleground of rural Georgia, as well as an undeniable beneficiary of affirmative action. Yet it was Justice Thomas who went well beyond even his conservative brethren on the court in 2009, declaring that the pre-clearance provisions of the landmark 1965 Voting Rights Act should be held unconstitutional, because they represented "punishment for long-past sins…an encroachment on states' rights." Thomas wrote that upholding the 1965 Voting Rights Act would legitimize "outdated assumptions about racial attitudes in covered jurisdictions." With friends like that, who needed enemies? Eight years later, the minority became the majority, and Justice Thomas' wish came true.

One cannot help but notice that what passes for civil rights controversies today seems worlds away from those of my generation. The nation's most highly-publicized racial cause celebre of the past few years was probably the case of the Jena Six, in which black high school students in LaSalle Parish, Louisiana—quite close to my old stomping grounds—were unfairly singled out for overzealous prosecution by the veteran, old-school local prosecutor. A hopeless romantic, I was on board; I wore my fading "Free The Jena Six" T-shirt. But let's face it: this was not exactly "Bloody Sunday" in Selma. Only one of the six youths ever served jail time, and it was the white student involved in the incident who was beaten unconscious. The controversial fatal shooting of young Trayvon Martin in Sanford, Florida in 2012 resulted in similar public outcry and demonstrations—justifiably so. However, in this case, his assailant was Hispanic—indeed, things are a bit more complicated these days.

Many of these contemporary causes célèbres—as unpleasant as they are in this day and age—are essentially matters of politically incorrect language or racial or ethnic insensitivity, rather than civil rights violations subject to legal remedy. Make no mistake: the gratuitously provocative remarks of Don Imus, The Greaseman, Rush Limbaugh, and their loudmouthed colleagues are disgusting. I would be delighted if they vanished from the airwaves forever. But however vile, such remarks are protected by the First Amendment, and in a country of over 300 million people, their ilk will always be with us.

It has been a long time since I have heard a white person utter the word "nigger," a frequently spoken and written term during my travels back in the day. But I now hear it regularly from black students at our local high school, and from African-American recording artists. These utterances are no less contemptible for the ethnic make-up of the speakers, but they are still constitutionally protected. The law has come a long way in protecting citizens registering to vote, or entering restaurants, from being attacked due to their race, but it is unrealistic to think that we will ever secure the right not to be offended.

Perhaps the most significant change in how we view the world of civil rights has been the relative decrease in importance of the historic black-white dichotomy, and the gradual rise of multiculturalism. Except for the Corpus Christi school desegregation litigation and several fatal police brutality matters in Texas and Puerto Rico, my civil rights cases involved the immoral and illegal denial of African-American citizens' rights by white public officials and private individuals. To my colleagues and I, this was a direct continuation of the original civil rights battles of the 1960's. But today's situation is far more complex. Foreign and domestic immigration in both the South and the nation as a whole have dramatically changed the demographics and the issues. In today's rural Southern and Midwestern communities, scarce jobs are sought after by Hispanics and Asians as well as black and white workers. Urban community conflicts often come down to African American vs. Hispanic, or upper middle class vs. working poor. Socially conservative African American clergy have often expressed strong opposition to the rights of gay citizens, perhaps the most volatile civil rights issue in today's world. American Indian tribal authorities form alliances with wealthy business interests to lobby legislatures for gaming licenses. Asian and African American organizations take different sides in some states in higher education admissions controversies. And ethnic groups are all over the map when it comes to immigration policy.

Even much of our language and cultural references—what we talk about when we talk about civil rights—often no longer makes much sense. An often-used example of the continuing legacy of legal segregation is the difficulty that African Americans experience in hailing taxicabs. Yet, as the female lead in the film "She's The One" declared in frustration to her cabdriver boyfriend: "You must be the only white, English-speaking taxicab driver in New York City!"

How true. I have taken many taxis in New York, Washington, and other cities over the years, but I can't recall any white American drivers. Discrimination certainly still exists, and it must be fought with all of our power. But we do ourselves no favors if we use the terms and strategies of a bygone age.

There is another important reason why it seems so difficult to recapture the urgency and righteousness of the old civil rights era. Historically, reforms, even revolutions, generally have taken place not when conditions are most desperate, but when hopes are on the rise. We often forget that, despite the seemingly nonstop social, cultural, and political upheaval, the 1960s were a time of considerable prosperity in America. Especially in the first half of the decade, the economy was growing steadily, and jobs were plentiful. This was still the era of the great post-war boom, when we were unchallenged as an industrial power. The Soviet Union, our great political rival, had yet to fully recover from the military and economic ravages of World War II, like the other major powers, both victors and vanquished. It was an era of American optimism, the zenith of the American Century, as exemplified by the

Race for Space. As the White House was well aware, we could no longer permit our international image to be sullied by satellite transmissions around the world of children in Alabama being attacked by police dogs and fire hoses.

Today our national mood is far different. Our economy is just beginning to recover from its lowest point since the Great Depression of the 1930s. People concerned about the security and size of their paychecks don't spend much time worrying about equal employment opportunity. We are now plagued by a series of seemingly intractable foreign conflicts that we would have once easily surmounted. Some would say we have become a more individualistic, narcissistic, even selfish society. The ideals of community, or a thriving public sector, are no longer in the forefront of our minds. In terms of civil rights consciousness, the present time seems more like the economically ruinous 1930s or the war-torn '40s, when developments were relatively symbolic, in the form of Marian Anderson's 1939 Lincoln Memorial concert and Jackie Robinson breaking baseball's color line in 1947. Still, as we have learned over time, sometimes progress takes unforeseen forms, and strikes when least anticipated.

Some would hold that traditional civil rights activism is no longer necessary, in light of the progress we have made. There is much to be said for this view; certainly there are many concrete, visible examples. Many times each year I fly, for business and pleasure, out of Baltimore's Thurgood Marshall International Airport. Like many icons of the movement, Marshall is now seen, especially by younger generations, as a universally beloved figure. But that wasn't always the case. A Maryland native and excellent student, he attended law school at Washington D.C.'s Howard University when the University of Maryland rejected him due to the prevailing Jim Crow policy of the day. He was my legal role model; I met him when he spoke at a law school forum, and, with my colleagues, I attended his wake in the Great Hall of the Supreme Court. The threats, attacks, indignities, and challenges he endured—with fabled good humor—make my tribulations seem trivial in comparison. As much as Dr. King or anyone else, he was the true hero of the civil rights movement. The dragons that Justice Marshall slew would have recoiled in horror to think that a major airport—and other public facilities—would one day be named in his honor.

Two years ago, in Albany, Georgia, site of some of the most brutal counterattacks of the early civil rights battles, a bronze statue of native son Ray Charles, the founding father of soul music, was dedicated in the town plaza. In 1979, Brother Ray's version of Hoagie Carmichael's classic "Georgia on My Mind" was named the official state song. These events are taken for granted by the young. But when I recount these stories before playing the tune for my more senior audiences, there are knowing nods and smiles—these folks never thought the day would ever come.

Philadelphia, Mississippi, which will forever be linked to the horrific murders of James Chaney, Andrew Goodman, and Mickey Schwerner that shocked the nation in 1964, not long ago elected James Young, an African American, as mayor. He was elected with a large number of white as well as black votes. Perhaps now, it is this southern Philadelphia that is the true City of Brotherly Love.

And who could ever have predicted this true story, retold by author Roy Blount, Jr. in The *Oxford American*:

> "Bill Nunn [African American scout for the National Football League's Pittsburgh Steelers, and father of actor Bill Nunn, Jr.] told me: He ran out of gas in a little town in Mississippi. A local white man drove up with his wife in the car, stopped, and asked Bill if he could help. Bill said he'd appreciate a ride to the gas station. The man said sure, jump in. He was just as friendly and helpful as he could be, and Bill told a local black man that the white man had certainly been nice. "Yep,' said the black man. "And the thing about it is, it was his brother killed Emmett Till."

Don't tell me things don't change.

༄

The above developments might arguably be dismissed as anecdotal, or few and far between. But not so the stunning, historic election of Barack Obama in November, 2008. This was The Shot Heard 'Round The World, or, in the words of a gathering of shell-shocked NAACP veterans at a Florida civil rights memorial service one month later, Judgment Day. Few saw it coming, and it is still so recent and unprecedented as to defy facile generalization or interpretation. History's verdict may be premature, but to most commentators to date, foreign and domestic, America is not, and never will be, the same place again:

Bob Herbert, New York Times national affairs columnist, November 8, 2008: "The nation deserves to take a bow. This is not the same place it used to be."

Bishop Desmond Tutu, South African Nobel Laureate:

> "The election of Barack Obama has turned America's image on its head. Today Africans walk taller than they did a week ago—just as they did when Nelson Mandela became South Africa's first black president in 1994. If a dark-skinned person can become the leader of the world's most powerful nation, what is to stop children everywhere from aiming for the stars?"

Barack Obama, 44th President of the United States:

> "There is an entire generation that will grow up taking for granted that the highest office in the land is filled by an African American. I mean, that is a radical thing. It changes how black children look at themselves. It also changes how white children look at black children. And I wouldn't underestimate the force of that. If there is anyone out there who still doubts that America is a place where all things are possible, who still wonders if the dream of our founders is alive in our time, who still questions the power of our democracy, tonight is your answer."

Indeed, from this moment on, why should anything short of the sky ever be the limit of expectations for a black child—any child—growing up in America? We have an African-American President; a black Attorney General as chief law enforcement officer; and a Puerto Rican woman sitting on the highest court in the land. For the first time, can we now utter the words "post-racial society" with a straight face?

⁓

If only it were that simple. Despite undeniable progress on the ground, and the spectacular triumph of President Obama, serious challenges remain. But perhaps they are not properly called civil rights challenges, with the images of marches, sit-ins, and appeals to the national conscience which that phrase implies. Those are the tactics of another era. For one thing, there will soon be no traditional "majority" to appeal to, as the demographic trends continue and the white population no longer outnumbers the rest of the country. And what good do marches do in the face of community-based crises like unacceptable school dropout rates; medical emergencies such as HIV, diabetes and other serious diseases; and a crumbling family structure in which over two-thirds of black children are born out of wedlock? Are sit-ins likely to affect the persistent, well-deserved feelings of mistrust and hostility toward police and the criminal justice system in minority communities—especially when the police department and courts in question are often led by minorities?

Focusing on these more complex issues—rather than the traditional robed and hooded targets I did battle with in my younger days—is sometimes characterized as "blaming the victim." Maybe so—but to me, civil rights and equal justice are not theoretical, academic concepts to be tailored for politically correct discussion. They are often matters of life and death, integral to our sense of national purpose, which should be treated in light of whatever approaches—traditional, innovative, or some combination of the two—have the best chance of succeeding. As President Obama emphasized in his speech to the NAACP's centennial convention:

> *"No matter how bitter the road or how stony the road, we have persevered. We have not faltered, nor have we grown weary. As Americans, we have demanded, strived for, and shaped a better destiny. That is what we are called to do once more. It will not be easy. It will take time. Doubts may rise and hopes recede. But if John Lewis could brave billy clubs to cross a bridge, then I know young people today can do their part to lift up our communities. If Emmett Till's uncle Moses Wright could summon the courage to testify against the men who killed his nephew, I know we can be better fathers and brothers, mothers and sisters in our own*

families. If three civil rights workers in Mississippi—black and white, Christian and Jew, city-born and country-bred—could lay down their lives in freedom's cause, I know we can come together to face down the challenges of our own time. We can fix our schools, heal our sick, and rescue our youth from violence and despair."

These are surely daunting problems, but they can and must be addressed. There has been no shortage of proposed plans of attack, and an army of predominantly—but not completely—young citizens of all creeds and colors can be mobilized for this campaign, just as in the electoral. But fresh, innovative goals and strategies are imperative to achieve anything other than paper victories. As African American professor and author Shelby Steele noted, the problem to be remedied in New Haven is not intentional discrimination, but the fact that black firefighters did so poorly on the promotion exam. Similarly, the ultimate solution to the admittedly unfair disparity between sentencing statutes for crack and powder forms of cocaine is not to equalize sentencing, but to mount a full-scale attack on the scourge of drug-addiction which has devastated so many predominantly-black communities. Washington, D.C.'s former reform school superintendent, Michele Rhee, was harshly criticized for proposing school closings which would assign students to schools on the "turf" of different crews or gangs, inviting violence, and there was merit to this criticism. But for God's sake, we should be mobilizing all of our resources so that no child has to deal with such an outrageous situation, rather than tailoring attendance policy to it. This is 21st-century America, not Baghdad after the overthrow of Saddam Hussein.

The need for new focus has been recognized by a legion of experts whose credentials and motivation cannot easily be questioned.

Civil rights historian and commentator Juan Williams, biographer of Justice Marshall and author of the powerful written accompaniment to the "Eyes On The Prize" civil rights documentary series, argues convincingly for a major community revitalization effort in his 2006 book, Enough. The legendary Robert P. Moses, who endured an unparalleled degree of physical and emotional suffering in the early Mississippi voter registration campaigns, led a nationwide effort to increase mathematical literacy among minority students. Above all, it is critical that the traditional, anti-discrimination tactics of the NAACP and similar organizations not be viewed as in conflict with the community improvement approach. There are plenty of resources to draw on for both battles; there is no reason—other than a purely academic one—for a replay of the Booker T. Washington vs. W.E.B. DuBois debate of a century ago. In the words of Bob Herbert of The New York Times:

> *"Addressing issues of values and behavior within the black community should not in any way imply a lessening of the pressure on the broader society to meet its legal and ethical obligations. It should be seen as an essential counterpoint to that pressure."*

﹏

There is another lingering dimension to the legacy of slavery and discrimination: the psychological. This is a compelling issue in the African-American community, many of whose members continue to view the world—President Obama's election notwithstanding—from a different perspective than others. A young black attorney recently told me that she is "working for The Man" at a federal agency, despite the reign of a black President and Attorney General. Black and white reaction to the arrest of Harvard Professor Henry Louis Gates were strikingly different; many whites blamed Gates' "aggressive attitude," even though he was apprehended for "breaking into" his own home. To the overwhelming majority of African-Americans, this was yet another example of racially selective police harassment. Witness the marked outcries of black satisfaction with the acquittal of O.J. Simpson, who never lifted a finger for the black community, and spent much of his adult life seeking the approval of wealthy white celebrities.

So many black citizens sadly still see themselves, and are seen by others, as outsiders. They are still often treated as The Other, even within the spectrum of minority populations. Asians are not grilled at polling places under the guise of "ballot security" on election day; no one is stopped by the police for "driving while Jewish." Italian and Irish Americans are not followed by security guards in department stores. The streets don't buzz with concerns about property values when a gay couple moves into the neighborhood. A black attorney colleague explained this to me quite straightforwardly, "It's different for us, and it always will be. We've got no place to hide."

As Reverend Wiley Shaw told me in Oakdale, Louisiana: hear too many insults, labels, and low expectations, and the anger inevitably turns inward as well as external. Witness the hideous, self-hating disfigurement of music icon Michel Jackson, whom African American Washington Post columnist Courtland Milloy characterized as a black man who wanted to look like a white Diana Ross. Hence the "crabs in a barrel" phenomenon, which my fellow musicians often speak of, whereby black musicians are victims of at least as much jealousy and cutthroat competition from their African American compatriots as from whites. Notes Etan Thomas, poet and professional basketball player, "Yes, we've been done wrong, but we do each other worse."

How heartbreaking, this insidious, internalized legacy of slavery and discrimination. And once again, the solution, if one exists, lies somewhere beyond any knowledge or experience that I might possess.

༄

So we carry on, buoyed by once unimaginable electoral success, but facing challenges more complex and subjective than those of an earlier, simpler time. It is time for a fresh, candid look at these old struggles, for there lie valuable lessons for the task at hand. Santayana's old bromide still holds: those who don't study history are doomed to repeat it. American civil rights history, as commonly recounted and taught today, consists in great measure of a series of myths, aimed at making a highly contentious, often violent period—when many people sat safely on the sidelines, and no small number were on the wrong side of history— more palatable. If this seems like an exaggeration, recall the shock of that university student at watching film of segregated bus transportation.

The myth of dedicated soldiers like Rosa Parks as simple pawns who happened to be in the right place at the right time: what nonsense! Mrs. Parks was a tireless worker for freedom long before the Montgomery bus boycott. She was a veteran member, and eventually secretary, of her local NAACP chapter, and participated in events protesting the murder of Emmett Till in neighboring Mississippi. She received training in progressive community organizing at the Highlander Folk School in

Tennessee.

The myth of early champions of freedom and equality as delusional, dangerous zealots: why is John Brown, who actually tried to do something concrete about slavery rather than just speak against it, always portrayed as a "religious fanatic?" Why are leaders of slave rebellions like Nat Turner and Denmark Vesey called emotionally disturbed? Why are the members of Congress who pushed for a meaningful restoration of the political rights of African Americans during Reconstruction referred to as the "Radical Republicans"?

The "Great Man" theory of civil rights history: this viewpoint sees the movement as a "top-down" phenomenon, owing its successes primarily to a few all-powerful leaders, notably Martin Luther King. Take nothing away from Dr. King. In fact, one could make a very strong case that he was the greatest American of the 20th century (who else—Franklin or Eleanor Roosevelt?). But the civil rights struggle was in fact the ultimate people's movement, in which thousands upon thousands of ordinary Americans, black and white, came together to speak truth to power. There would have been a civil rights movement without Dr. King, but there would have been no Martin Luther King Holiday without the civil rights movement. We need not wait for divine prophets to inspire us to change our world. That power still exists within ourselves, if we choose to use it.

The myth of King as a cautious, middle-of-the-road leader: in reality, Dr. King was an intellectually rigorous, fearless proponent of radical social change across a broad range of issues. He was an early, vocal opponent of American policy in Vietnam, to the dismay of a great many more cautious civil rights leaders. He was a determined strategist for economic justice, organizing coalitions of workers across racial lines. Dr. King's goal was not just an integrated, but a fundamentally transformed, America.

The myth of the Neanderthal Klansman as leader of the opposition: of course the Samuel Bowerses and James Earl Rays deserved all the opprobrium they received. But it was the ruling power structure, in the form of institutions such as the Mississippi State Sovereignty Commission and southern-dominated Congressional Democrats, who propped up the system of segregation for so many years. The redneck villains portrayed in "Mississippi Burning" and similar Hollywood dramas were the popular bogeymen, but ultimately they served as convenient pawns in the greater political power game.

The myth of the pro-civil rights religious community: how we could have used this in our time in the South! But the truth was far closer to King's famous description of 11 a.m. on Sunday morning as the nation's most segregated hour. William Faulkner, that rare southern luminary who predicted the coming civil rights crisis well before it gathered momentum, pointed out that the clergy's silence on such an overriding moral issue was particularly egregious in the South, "where everyone goes to church." And he wasn't just talking about the numerically-dominant Southern Baptists, who had to be convinced through a personal visit that John Kennedy's Catholicism did not pose a mortal threat to the country. For example: when Rosa Parks was invited to attend the Montgomery wedding of Lucy Durr, her friend and occasional employer, she was told by officials of St. John's Episcopal Church that she could do so only if she dressed as a servant.

The southern synagogues were not much better. Although a rare presence in rural communities, many southern cities had old-line congregations of predominantly German Jews of mid-19th century origin, who had become as carefully establishment-oriented as possible, given the prevailing anti-Semitism in the region and the country as a whole. In my experiences, which are consistent with the historical record, southern Catholic churches and many of their individual members were considerably more supportive of anti-segregation efforts. Many Catholic dioceses refused to allow their parochial schools to serve as "white flight" refuges when public school desegregation began, and at least one Catholic opponent of civil rights, the notorious racist Leander Perez, powerful political boss of Plaquemines Parish, Louisiana (who personally arrested my friend, pioneer civil rights attorney Richard Sobol), was excommunicated from the Church.

Many northern religious organizations, although far from monolithic on the issue, were generally supportive of the movement—certainly none more so than the Jewish community. It was no accident that Andrew Goodman and Mickey Schwerner met their deaths along with James Chaney in Mississippi, nor that Dr. King and Ralph Abernathy joined hands with Abraham Heschel and Maurice Eisendrath in the front row of the 1965 march in Selma. Jews from up north streamed south in absolutely astonishing numbers to participate in every aspect of the movement, and they often recruited additional volunteers upon returning home. I will never forget the sight of our rabbi, Sidney Akselrad, reporting to our small California congregation on his experiences in Alabama and Mississippi, his head still bandaged from the violent blows he had received.

The myth of civil rights as a gradual, generally accepted historical process: far from steady, America's path to equal opportunity has been one of fits and starts, with long intervals of slumber punctuated by rare spasms of activism. Following the Civil War and the passage of the 13th, 14th, and 15th Amendments, a century of racial retrenchment and the reign of Jim Crow settled in, enforced behind closed doors by public officials, while the Ku Klux Klan and their comrades took care of the necessary dirty work. Precious little progress took place until the 1960s, which were followed by forty years of not-always-so-benign neglect until the 2008 election of Barack Obama.

The legacy of the civil rights struggle is a profound one for the nation, with many concrete and potential beneficiaries. One theory—and there is considerable evidence to support it—holds that no one profited more from the end of legalized segregation than the southern white population. The end of violent confrontations brought at least some semblance of stability to the region, paving the way for much-needed outside business investment and the beginning of the end of the South as an underdeveloped country in our midst. On a local level, many a merchant profited nicely by being "forced" to serve all customers, and municipalities saved many dollars previously devoted to needlessly-duplicative segregated facilities.

On a grander scale, the movement's triumphs set a shining example for other groups seeking their right to pursue the American dream. Few, if any, people were ever as historically demonized and disenfranchised as African-Americans—yet they slew Goliath and cast off their chains, at least the legal ones. What an indelible message for their brothers and sisters: if you're of Hispanic or Asian heritage, you don't have to muffle your native language or be ashamed to celebrate your cultural holidays. If you're a young schoolgirl, you can grow up to be anything you want to be, not just the traditional "women's occupations." If you're gay, you don't have to spend your life in denial, cowering in the darkness of the closet. If you use a wheelchair, you can still attend that concert, that ball-game, or that presidential inauguration. This is your country too.

What a cruel, perverse travesty this entire history of discrimination is premised upon a scientifically discredited theory of racial superiority. Indeed, the entire concept of "race" now rests on quicksand in the harsh light of unassailable genetic research. We may well be on the path toward redemption, but it comes too late for all the tragic victims of a twisted, anti-democratic value system that will not soon be forgotten. As for the perpetrators: the time is long past for Lincoln's lofty proscription of "malice toward none."

For those who wore the robes and hoods, pulled the triggers, lit the fuses, and wielded the axe-handles, justice can never come too late. The Justice Department's Civil Rights Division, where I toiled back in the day, still holds open a number of notorious, unsolved cases similar to those from my own docket. No matter how old or infirm, like their Nazi war-criminal counterparts in exile around the world, these destroyers of the American Dream must be made to pay the piper.

And what of all the well-educated public officials, religious leaders, educators, and others who could blame neither poverty nor ignorance? They had no excuses. From J. Edgar Hoover, who remained ever relentless in his torment and character assassination of Martin Luther King and other civil rights leaders; to Ronald Reagan, who vigorously opposed every piece of civil rights legislation, scandalously commenced his presidential campaign with a call for "states' rights" in infamous Philadelphia, Mississippi, and insulted King's memory when he reluctantly signed the King Holiday legislation into law; to Jerry Falwell, Pat Robertson, and their brethren of the cloth, who shamelessly twisted their Savior's message of love and brotherhood into justification for bigotry. They ignored every opportunity to lead rather than follow; to reason rather than inflame; to include rather than exclude; to love rather than hate. They should have known better.

God may well have mercy on their souls. But in my most mortal eyes, they remain The Unforgiven.

Howard L. Feinstein

Epilogue: Amazing Grace

> *Ye shall tread down the wicked; for they shall be ashes under the soles of your feet...And He shall turn the heart of the fathers to the children, and the heart of the children to their fathers.*
>
> Malachi 4: 3, 6

The murders of Harry and Harriette Moore faded over time, but they were not quite forgotten. In the final years of the twentieth century, the inevitable ripples from the civil rights revolution slowly but surely brought some small degree of change to Florida's north coast. And early in the new century, other cold cases from the horrors of the movement's tumultuous days were revived. Hopes were raised, although they had been raised and dashed before.

In the wake of the public furor over the bombing, the FBI opened an investigation. There were many interviews, many meetings, many pieces of evidence obtained, but the dots were never connected. The Ku Klux Klan network in the area remained strong, and anyone tempted to provide useful information to the Feds would be paid a visit from his or her local Klavern. The wagons were circled, and the climate of fear was pervasive. As Frank Meech, an FBI agent assigned to the investigation, explained: "They knew our car, they knew where we were. You couldn't move without them knowing it…People said 'Hell no, I won't testify. I'd be dead tomorrow.' "

Of course, I came to know this feeling all too well. In addition, local police and sheriff's departments, usually close working partners with the Bureau, were incredulous that the federal government was taking the matter so seriously. As Meech recalled: "We'd go in and talk to someone in law enforcement, and they'd say, 'what the hell are you investigating that for? He was only a nigger.' "

To no one's surprise, the federal investigation was closed, with no action taken.

The Florida Department of Law Enforcement conducted an investigation in 1991, and again in 2003. No charges were filed in either inquiry. Between the two state investigations, Florida State University professor Ben Green wrote a comprehensive study of the case, *Before His Time—The Untold Story Of Harry T. Moore, America's First Civil Rights Martyr*. Green's book included several promising leads, and it received attention locally and in academic circles, helping to keep the flame of remembrance alive a while longer. Finally, shortly before Christmas of 2004, the Florida Attorney General's Office announced the state's intention to launch an exhaustive re-opening of the case. With few persons involved still alive, and no apparent new sources of physical evidence, this seemed like the last possible opportunity for justice.

∽

In late fall of 2005, a colleague of my wife, knowing of my civil rights background, forwarded to me a letter and packet of materials from a member of her church. It was the carefully prepared and organized story of a tragic bombing in Florida in 1951, concluding in a plea for justice and recognition all these years later. My interest was piqued, but my cynical legal training immediately kicked in. My courtroom days might be over, but I still received regular calls seeking free legal advice; spinning tales of injustice and desired revenge; and always, the conspiracy theories. At first glance, this sounded suspiciously like the latter. I had spent a huge amount of time investigating and litigating civil rights cases in every corner of Florida; surely I would have heard some rumor, some reference to a tale this compelling. But, remarkably, it all checked out. Not just the basic outline, but the dates, the places, and the names—it was all accurate and meticulously documented.

I'll be damned: Faulkner was right. The past is never dead. It's not even past. An unknown force, beyond my power to control or resist, dialed the phone number of a living ghost, Juanita Evangeline Moore, and together we journeyed backward to a place and time we were powerless to escape.

She was a petite, proud woman in her seventies. Her hearing, vision, and comprehension were every bit as good as mine. She was impeccably dressed, sometimes in a fashionable African print dress, sometimes in more traditional church attire. She spoke with the measured quality and grammatical perfection of a veteran diplomat. She possessed none of the wild-eyed fervor, the defensiveness, the "transmit only" conversational style of the paranoid true believer. Her compact, one-bedroom garden apartment was a graceful, respectful, but not garish or overdone, memorial to her martyred parents, their classically framed portraits gazing down from the wall with the wisdom and guidance on which she still relied.

Their martyrdom had become her lifelong mission, but she was also a productive citizen, one of Washington's legions of retired civil servants, still lending an experienced, compassionate hand to others in need. Her knowledge of civil rights history extended far beyond her own family's story. I could hardly name a person or place from my southern journeys past that she didn't recognize. When she spoke to my congregation, she held that ordinarily tumultuous, questioning bunch in a state of stunned silence, culminating in a thunderous burst of applause. She was a ghost come alive.

JUANITA EVANGELINE MOORE IN HER OWN WORDS

I was coming home two days after Christmas. When I got off the train, this is what hit me in the face: Your father's dead;

your mother's in the hospital. What kind of Christmas do you think I had? What kind of Christmases do you think I still have? I just want the world to know what happened to my dad ... I've paid a price, mentally and physically. I've had depression and stress-related ailments. It's been lonely, and I'm still lonely. Everything I do, I first ask myself what my mom and dad would think. After my father was killed, and my mother lay dying, I said 'I hate all white people.' But my aunt told me, 'That's not how your father taught you. Never use that word "hate." It will never help achieve your father's goals.' I know I was a bitter person. I did all this work myself. The NAACP did nothing. No civil rights organizations did. They want to preserve the myth that the civil rights movement started with Martin Luther King and Rosa Parks. I believe in God seriously. That's kept me from being hateful, mean, and vindictive.... God's taken care of the people who did this. He has dealt with them very, very badly, and they will continue to be prosecuted His way.

∼

August 16, 2006—Mims, Florida: Attorney General (later Governor) Charlie Crist announced that, after extensive investigation, the state had sufficient evidence to secure the indictment of four Klansmen in the 1951 bombing death of Harry and Harriette Moore. The evidence showed that Earl J. Brooklyn possessed floor plans to the Moore home, and recruited three others for the bombing plot. Joseph N. Cox placed the bomb under the Moores' bedroom. The other named conspirators were Tillman H. Belvin—like Brooklyn and Cox, a former member of the Georgia KKK, my old nemesis—and Edward L. Spivey, "exalted Cyclops" in the hideous hierarchy of his local Klavern. The evidence indicated that the collection taken up by the Klan helped to pay off the mortgages of Cox and Belvin. In 1951 on Florida's north coast, Thirty Pieces of Silver = $5,000.

But there would be no indictments. As Juanita Evangeline Moore prophesied, God had dealt with the conspirators very badly. Brooklyn and Belvin died of natural causes within one year of the bombing. Cox committed suicide in 1952, the day after he was interviewed by the FBI. Spivey was tormented with guilt, and periodically hinted of his and Cox's complicity in the bombing. He finally succumbed to cancer in 1980.

∽

Today, at the site of the bombing, stands the Harry T. and Harriette V. Moore Memorial Park and Cultural Center, on Freedom Avenue. This is due to the tireless, half-century long quest for justice by Juanita Evangeline Moore, who returns every December to lead a memorial service. She keeps the dream alive through a busy schedule of speaking appearances, not only to honor her father, but on behalf of all those who shared his struggle. Seven months before the case was legally put to rest, she delivered a stirring address to an audience, Christian and Jewish, black and white, at the Holocaust Memorial Resource and Education Center of Central Florida:

> *"Sometimes, I refer to him as a twentieth century Moses. I call your attention to the Book of Exodus, Chapter 3, Verse 10: 'Therefore, come now and I will send you to Pharaoh, so that you may bring my people, the sons of Israel, out of Egypt.'"*

Like Martin Luther King, who followed in her father's footsteps, she is a devout Christian, invoking the words of the Old Testament prophets in the universal cause of justice and freedom. And like her fellow prophets, she paid a price.

∼

Postscript:

December 14, 2008—Mims, Florida: On a gray afternoon in a tiny town in north Florida, a world away from the nearby multitudes streaming south like migratory birds for the holidays, a quiet crowd gathers in a roadside churchyard, at twin graves marked with simple, yet elegant, headstones. In attendance are members of the Florida House and Senate; representatives from the Governor's office; Brevard County elected officials; statewide NAACP officers; men and women of the cloth; and, as always, Juanita Evangeline Moore and her family and friends. The mourners silently place wreaths and flowers at the graves. Every year they gather here, to commemorate the lives of the martyred couple.

But this year is special. Not just because the Killers Of The Dream have at long last been identified. Not just because today the groundbreaking ceremony will take place for the Harry and Harriette Moore Home Replica Construction. But because, in one month, an event will take place in Washington, D.C., that even an incurable optimist like Harry Moore could not have believed would happen. The people of Mims, and surely throughout the south, are still in shock over what they and their fellow citizens have wrought. It is the culmination of a battle begun so long ago, when the Moore family drove dangerous backcountry roads to make the right to vote a reality. Indeed, when he takes the oath of office, the new President will acknowledge that he stands on the shoulders of those before him who laid the groundwork for this day—surely none broader than those of Harry Moore.

So this year, when we gather to sing and pray in the graveyard, the tears are not only from sadness, but of joy:

For the lives and work of Harry T. and Harriette Moore, we thank thee, Lord. Because we are the beneficiaries of Harry T. Moore's work, we thank thee, Lord, and on this day, we humbly petition that you will continue to grant us your favor as we continue to multiply the work that Mr. Moore has started.

Amen.

Fire on the Bayou

Coda

These days, I dance around the edges of the world of civil rights. I write about it. I give lectures and lead discussions about it. I teach it to those with an interest in such things. I provide some measure of aid and comfort to victims of discrimination whose paths cross mine. But I am essentially on the sidelines, an observer and commentator, no longer putting myself on the line. That was another person, another time.

Howard L. Feinstein

Notes and Sources

Prologue: The Horror

1. Introductory quotation: Joseph Conrad, *Under Western Eyes* (1911) Modern Library ed., 2001 – p. 113

2. Much of the material in the Prologue and Epilogue is based on interviews, telephone conversations, and meetings with Juanita Evangeline Moore. Historical events noted by Ms. Moore were independently corroborated.

3. The reference to slavery is not metaphorical. Forced agricultural labor still exists in the United States, and the Civil Rights Division's Criminal Section has continued to prosecute those cases, including several in Florida. The applicable federal statutes are at Title 18, U.S. Code, Chapter 77.

4. The St. Augustine campaign, in which many, including Martin Luther King, were jailed, is comprehensively recounted in volume two

of Taylor Branch's masterful civil rights trilogy: *Pillar of Fire* (Simon & Schuster: 1998), chapters 3, 24-25, 27. Many years after his courageous participation in minor league baseball in the South, Jackie Robinson took part in the St. Augustine civil rights demonstrations.

5. The Supreme Court's landmark "white primary" decision was *Smith v. Allwright*, 321 U.S. 649 (1944). *Smith* held that Texas–like the rest of the South, effectively a one-party state–could not treat its Democratic party as if it were a private club.

6. The convictions of the Groveland Four were reversed in *Shepherd v. Florida*, 341 U.S. 50 (1951).

7. The influence and actions of the local Ku Klux Klan are described in the Report of the Florida Attorney General's office, Aug. 16, 2006. See Executive Summary and Press Release, at www.myfloridalegal.com/HarryMoore.

8. President Truman ordered the desegregation of the military in Executive Order 9981 (1948).

9. The Christmas night setting at the Moore home is from Report of the Florida Attorney General's Office, Aug. 16, 2006. Executive Summary, p. 8, n. 6.

10. The 1951 wave of racially motivated bombings, and the aftermath of the bombing of the Moore home in and beyond Mims, was reported in the Christian Science Monitor, Dec. 12, 1951; and Ebony magazine, April 12, 1952.

11. The verse is from "The Ballad of Harry T. Moore," from *The Collected Poems of Langston Hughes* (Alfred A. Knopf: 1995), pp. 588-90.

California Dreaming

12. The F. Scott Fitzgerald passage is from the conclusion of *The Great*

Gatsby (Charles Scribner's Sons: 1925).

13. William Faulkner's memorable phrase is from *Requiem for a Nun* (Random House: 1951).

14. The film "Plenty," directed by Fred Schepisi (Republic Studios – 1985) was based on David Hare's 1978 stage play of the same name.

15. Dr. Jamison writes of her experiences in *An Unquiet Mind* (Alfred A. Knopf: 1995).

16. Rev. Hoffman's story, and that of other holocaust survivors, is set forth in Kenneth Jacobson's *Embattled Selves* (Atlantic Monthly Press: 1994)

17. An informative look at Silicon Valley's unusual predicament can be found in "Google's Buses Help Its Workers Beat the Rush," by Miguel Haft, *New York Times*, March 10, 2007.

18. For the story of the economic boom and transformation of California during this time, see Ethan Rarick, California Rising: *The Life and Times of Pat Brown* (University of California Press: 2005)

19. There is a wealth of material on counterculture California. One book which rings very true is Kirse Granat May, *Golden State, Golden Youth – The California Image in Popular Culture, 1955-1966* (University of North Carolina Press: 2002). Highly recommended are the archives of *Rolling Stone* magazine from that period, when it was located in San Francisco.

20. "We Want The World And We Want it Now": The lyrics are from the song "When The Music's Over", a '60s anthem by The Doors on the album "Strange Days" (Elektra Records – 1967).

21. For an interesting look at the arrival of baseball in California as metaphor for the state's rise to national prominence, see Jane Leavy, Sandy Koufax: *A Lefty's Legacy* (HarperCollins: 2002).

22. This sad history is recalled in a "Where Are They Now" piece on Mays in the July 14-21, 2008 issue of Sports Illustrated. Mays, whose public image was definitely not that of a civil rights activist, could step up to the plate when necessary; he was a tireless mentor to young minority players (baseball had only been desegregated since 1947). He was also instrumental in quelling an incipient riot in the Hunter's Point area of San Francisco, which generally escaped the urban conflagrations that plagued many cities during the 1960's (see Charles Einstein's wonderful biography/memoir, *Willie's Time* (Lippincott: 1979).

23. Well before his masterful trilogy, *America In the King Years*, Taylor Branch coauthored Bill Russell's memoir, *Second Wind* (Random House: 1979).

24. The Supreme Court opinion in *Reitman v. Mulkey*, 387 U.S. 368 (1967), sets forth the history of this controversy in detail.

25. The widely acclaimed film "Easy Rider," directed by co-star Dennis Hopper (Columbia Pictures, 1969) is one of the outstanding depictions of 1960s counter-culture. It is also eerily reminiscent of my own journeys through the South as a naïve young Californian.

26. "If it feels good, do it" is one of the classic sixties youth-culture mantras. It is ascribed to various luminaries from that period, including radical agent provocateur Abby Hoffman and the great singer Janis Joplin, both of whom I heard in person several times.

Hitler at the Post Office

27. Like the murders of Chaney, Goodman, and Schwerner, racially-motivated killings were often triggered when the wrong people were spotted in vehicles with the wrong people at the wrong time. See the chilling account, in Taylor Branch's *At Canaan's Edge* (Simon & Schuster: 2006), pp. 172-179, of the shooting of Viola Liuzzo, who had gone South from

Michigan for the Selma, Alabama voting rights demonstrations in 1965.

28. The story of the Chaney, Goodman, and Schwerner murders is thoroughly recounted in *We Are Not Afraid*, by Seth Cagin and Philip Dray (Macmillan: 1982). The plan was carried out by a Ku Klux Klan contingent including clergymen and law enforcement officers. The case is still being pursued by the U.S. Department of Justice for possible prosecution of additional defendants.

29. The Mississippi State Sovereignty Commission was established by the state legislature in 1956. General Laws of the State of Mississippi, 1956 – Chapter 365, 520-524. The Commission's far-reaching, KGB-like powers, secret files, and informer networks were eventually exposed through lengthy federal court litigation. See *A.C.L.U. v. Fordice*, 969 F. Supp. 403 (S.D. Miss. 1994).

All-American City

30. While federal juvenile prosecutions are rare, with several procedural peculiarities, they are authorized by law. See Title 18, Sections 5031, 5032.

31. In *Virginia v. Black*, 538 U.S. 343 (2003), the Supreme Court emphasized the historic nature of the burning cross as a symbol of racial intimidation, holding that incidents such as that in South Williamsport were not protected by the First Amendment.

32. For an excellent account, with historical background, of an early twentieth century housing intimidation case in Detroit, see *Arc of Justice*, by Kevin Boyle (Holt: 2004).

33. Judge Muir's opinion was filed as: *In Re Juvenile Proceedings vs. John Doe*, Jr., Cr. No. 81-00156 (M. D. Pa. 1981).

34. *Klan-Destine Relationships – A Black Man's Odyssey in the Ku Klux Klan* (New Horizon Press: 1998) is available at Daryl Davis's website, www.

daryldavis.com.

The Long and Winding Road

35. The Mobile school desegregation case is *Davis v. Board of School Commissioners of Mobile County*, 318 F. 2nd 63 (5th Cir. 1963); 322 F.2d 356 (5th Cir. 1963.)

36. The Mobile school construction kickback case is noted in *New York Times*, Dec. 15, 1986.

37. The Houston school desegregation case is *Sampson v. Aldine Independent School District*, Civil Action No. 64-H-273 (S.D. Tex.). The school district was eventually declared "unitary" in 2004 by the federal district court.

38. The Cerro Maravilla events and their ramifications have been widely documented. Reports and transcripts of the hearings held by the Senate of Puerto Rico are available in Spanish. The appellate decisions affirming the convictions of the police officers are: *United States v. Reveron Martinez*, 836 F. 2d 684 (1st Cir. 1988) and *United States v. Moreno Morales*, 815 F.2d 725 (1st Cir. 1987).

39. The Corpus Christi school desegregation litigation was *Cisneros v. Corpus Christi Independent School District*, 324 F. Supp. 599 (S.D. Tex. 1970).

House-Hunting While Black

40. The affirmance by the United States Court of Appeals of the jury's guilty verdict is reported at 722 F.2d 92 (5th Cir. 1983).

41. Note: In Louisiana, counties are called parishes.

The Unforgiven

42. There has been a great deal of writing on the civil rights movement. Much of the early literature proved premature, incomplete, or so personal as to be of limited historical use. The passage of time has now provided sufficient perspective and previously inaccessible documentary sources. By far the gold standard in the field is Taylor Branch's magnificent trilogy, *America in the King Years* (Simon & Schuster): *Parting The Waters, 1954-63* (1988), *Pillar Of Fire, 1963-65* (1998); *At Canaan's Edge, 1965-68* (2006)

43. Rep. John Lewis's *Walking With The Wind* (Simon & Schuster: 1998) is a riveting personal history by a giant of the movement, and David Halberstam's *The Children* (Random House: 1998) is an excellent account of early demonstrations and protests in Tennessee.

44. "Eyes On the Prize – America's Civil Rights Movement" is highly recommended. It is available on videotape and DVD (P.B.S. Video: 2006).

45. The landmark Supreme Court decision declaring state anti-miscegenation laws unconstitutional is *Loving v. Virginia*, 388 U.S. 1 (1967).

46. The Nebraska law dividing Omaha into three ethnically identifiable school districts was introduced as Neb. Bill LB 1024 (2006).

47. The Supreme Court opinion in the Seattle and Louisville voluntary school integration cases is at 551 U.S. 701 (2007).

Epilogue: Amazing Grace

48. Much of the material in the Epilogue is based on interviews, telephone conversations and meetings with Juanita Evangeline Moore. Historical events mentioned by Ms. Moore were independently corroborated.

49. Special Agent Meech is quoted in one of the first investigative pieces on the Moore case, "The Haunting," by Karen Dukess and Richard Hart, in *Tropic* magazine, *Miami Herald*, Feb. 16, 1992.

50. Ben Green's book is *Before His Time – The Untold Story of Harry T.*

Moore, America's First Civil Rights Martyr (The Free Press: 1999).

51. "I was coming home..."—The quote is from the article "Civil Rights Activist Murders Site Excavated"—Dec. 3, 2005, at www.afrigeneas.com

52. The Florida Attorney General's office's investigative report, executive summary, and press release (August 16, 2006) are at www.myfloridalegal.com/HarryMoore. See also "Four Klan Members Linked to 1951 Bombing." Washington Post, Aug. 17, 2006 – A17.

53. The quotation is from Juanita Evangeline Moore's address at the Holocaust Memorial Resource and Education Center of Central Florida in Maitland, FL, Jan. 16, 2006.

Selected Civil Rights Timeline

1787—U.S. Constitution drafted. Slaves counted as 3/5 of free persons.

1857—*Dred Scott v. Sanford*: Supreme court rules slaves "personal property."

1859—John Brown's anti-slavery raid on federal armory at Harper's Ferry.

1861-1865—Civil War

1863—President Lincoln issues Emancipation Proclamation

1865—13th Amendment: Slavery and involuntary servitude prohibited.

1866—1866 Civil Rights Act: All persons born in U.S. are citizens, with right to enter into contracts, and buy and sell property (President Johnson's veto overridden).

1868—14th Amendment: All persons entitled to equal protection and due process of law.

1870—15th Amendment: Right to vote may not be denied on account of race.

1896—*Plessy v. Ferguson*: Supreme Court upholds "separate but equal" doctrine.

1920—19th Amendment: Right to vote may not be denied on account of sex.

1947—Jackie Robinson becomes Major League Baseball's first black player in modern era.

1948—President Truman issues Executive Order 9981, desegregating Armed Forces.

1951—NAACP leader Harry T. Moore and his wife, Harriette Moore, killed in Mims, Florida Ku Klux Klan bombing.

1954—*Brown v. Board of Education* I: Supreme Court prohibits segregated public schools (*Plessy* doctrine overruled).

1955—*Brown v. Board of Education* II: Supreme courts orders public schools desegregated "with all deliberate speed".

1955—Murder of 14-year-old Emmett Till in Mississippi.

1955—Rosa Parks launches Montgomery, Alabama bus boycott.

1957—Pres. Eisenhower sends federal troops to enforce Little Rock school desegregation.

1960—College students lead anti-segregation sit-ins in North Carolina, Tennessee, and Georgia.

1961—Freedom Riders' struggle to desegregate interstate bus lines.; 23rd

Amendment: District of Columbia residents granted right to vote in presidential elections.

1962—James Meredith becomes first black student at University of Mississippi, following violent uprising put down by federal troops.

1963—Four black children killed in Birmingham church bombing; school children lead Birmingham desegregation marches; civil rights leader Medgar Evers murdered in Mississippi; March on Washington for civil rights.

1964—Civil Rights workers James Chaney, Andrew Goodman, Michael Schwerner murdered in Mississippi; 24th Amendment: Poll taxes prohibited in federal elections; 1964 Civil Rights Act: Discrimination prohibited in public accommodations, employment, federal programs. Federal government authorized to enforce equal educational opportunity; *Heart of Atlanta Motel v. U.S.; Katzenbach v. McClung*: Supreme Court upholds constitutionality of public accommodations provisions of 1964 Civil Rights Act.

1965—Voting rights marches in Selma, Alabama; President Johnson issues Executive Order 11246, requiring affirmative action in federal contracts.; 1965 Voting Rights Act: Racial discrimination prohibited in all elections, enforceable by federal government.

1967—Loving v. Virginia: Supreme Court declares state prohibitions against interracial marriage unconstitutional.

1968—Martin Luther King assassinated; 1968 Fair Housing Act: Discrimination prohibited in sale, rental of housing.

1974—*Milliken v. Bradley*: Supreme Court holds unconstitutional use of metropolitan-wide desegregation remedy for segregated city public school district.

2007—Parents Involved In Community Schools v. Seattle School District No. 1: Supreme Court prohibits voluntary consideration of race to bring about enrollment diversity in public schools.

2008—Barack Obama elected 44th President of United States.

Applicable Federal Statutes

Civil actions by the Attorney General

Whenever the Attorney General receives a complaint in writing signed by a parent or group of parents to the effect that his or their minor children...are being deprived by a school board of the equal protection of the laws...and the Attorney General believes that the institution of an action will materially further the orderly achievement of desegregation in public education, the Attorney General is authorized ... to institute a civil action against such parties and for such relief as may be appropriate.

U.S. Code, Title 42, Section 2000c-6

Conspiracy against rights

If two or more persons conspire to injure, oppress, threaten, or intimidate any person…in the free exercise or enjoyment of any right or privilege secured to him by the constitution or laws of the United States; or

If two or more persons go in disguise on the highway, or on the premises of another, with intent to prevent or hinder his free exercise or enjoyment of any right or privilege so secured –

They shall be fined…or imprisoned not more than ten years, or both.

U.S. Code, Title 18, Section 241

Deprivation of rights under color of law

Whoever, under color of any law…willfully subjects any person to the deprivation of any rights…protected by the Constitution or laws of the United States or to different punishments, pains, or penalties…by reason of his color or race…shall be fined or imprisoned not more than one year, or both.

U.S. Code, Title 18, Section 242

Interference with federally-protected activities by force

Whoever, whether or not acting under color of law, by force or threat of force willfully injures, intimidates or interferes with, or attempts to injure, intimidate or interfere with…any person because of his race…and because he has been…enjoying employment by any private employer…shall be fined or imprisoned not more than one year, or both.

U.S. Code, Title 18, Section 245(b)(2)(c)

Mailing threatening communications

Whoever knowingly causes to be delivered by the Postal Service any communication…containing…any threat to injure the person of the addressee or of another shall be fined or imprisoned not more than five years, or both.

U.S. Code, Title 18, Section 876 (c)

Interference, coercion, or intimidation—fair housing

It shall be unlawful to coerce, intimidate, threaten, or interfere with any person in the exercise or enjoyment of...or on account of his having aided or encouraged any other person in the exercise or enjoyment of [Fair Housing].

U.S. Code, Title 42, Section 3617

Interference with fair housing by force

Whoever, whether or not acting under color of law, by force or threat of force willfully injures, intimidates or interferes with, or attempts to injure, intimidate or interfere with:

Any person because of his race...and because he is selling, purchasing, renting, financing, occupying... any dwelling, or affording another person opportunity or protection so as to participate [in these] activities...shall be fined or imprisoned not more than one year, or both.

U.S. Code, Title 42, Section 3631

Perjury

Whoever having taken an oath...that he will testify truly...and contrary to such oath states any material mater which he does not believe to be true...is guilty of perjury, and shall be fined or imprisoned not more than five years, or both.

U.S. Code, Title 18, Section 1621

False declarations before grand jury or court

Whoever under oath in any proceeding before…any court or grand jury of the United States knowingly makes any false material declaration…shall be fined or imprisoned not more than five years, or both.

U.S. Code, Title 18, Section 1623

Subornation of perjury

Whoever procures another to commit perjury is guilty of subornation of perjury, and shall be fined or imprisoned not more than five years, or both.

U.S. Code, Title 18, Section 1622

Obstruction of justice

Whoever corruptly or by threats or force, or by any threatening letters or communication, influences, obstructs, or impedes…the administration of justice, shall be … imprisoned for not more than 10 years or fined, or both.

U.S. Code, Title 18, Section 1503

CPSIA information can be obtained at www.ICGtesting.com
Printed in the USA
BVOW03s0331211114

376054BV00003B/6/P